The short guide to sociology

Mark Doidge
Rima Saini

First edition published in Great Britain in 2020 by

Policy Press
University of Bristol
1-9 Old Park Hill
Bristol BS2 8BB
UK
+44 (0)117 954 5940
pp-info@bristol.ac.uk
www.policypress.co.uk

North America office:
Policy Press
c/o The University of Chicago Press
1427 East 60th Street
Chicago, IL 60637, USA
t: +1 773 702 7700
f: +1 773-702-9756
sales@press.uchicago.edu
www.press.uchicago.edu

© Policy Press 2020

British Library Cataloguing in Publication Data
A catalogue record for this book is available from the British Library.

Library of Congress Cataloging-in-Publication Data
A catalog record for this book has been requested.

ISBN 978-1-4473-5240-2 paperback
ISBN 978-1-4473-5241-9 ePub
ISBN 978-1-4473-5243-3 ePdf

The right of Mark Doidge and Rima Saini to be identified as the authors of this work has been
asserted by them in accordance with the Copyright, Designs and Patents Act 1988.

Cover design by Qube Design Associates, Bristol
Front cover image: istock
Printed and bound by CPI Group (UK) Ltd, Croydon, CR0 4YY

Contents

List of boxes and figures

Boxes

Figures

About the authors

Mark Doidge is Senior Research Fellow in the School of Sport and Service Management at the University of Brighton. He is also currently a trustee of the British Sociological Association and convenor of the Sport Study Group. His current research focuses on the role of sport and leisure in supporting refugees and asylum seekers. Dr Doidge's research also focuses on political activism among football fans across Europe, particularly anti-racism, supporting refugees, anti-discrimination, anti-violence, and the broader political identities associated with football fandom. He is the author of *Ultras: The Passion and Performance of Contemporary Football Fandom* (2020 forthcoming, Manchester University Press, with Kossakowski and Mintert), *Football Italia: Italian Football in an Age of Globalization* (2015, Bloomsbury), *Collective Action and Football Fandom: A Relational Sociological Approach* (2018, Palgrave Macmillan, with Cleland, Millward and Widdop); and co-editor of *Sociologists' Tales* (2015, Policy Press, with Twamley and Scott) and *Transforming Sport: Knowledges, Practices, Structures* (2018, Routledge, with Carter and Burdsey).

Rima Saini is Lecturer in Sociology at the University of Middlesex. She completed a PhD in quantitative sociology at City, University of London in 2019, following an MSc in social research methods (City, University of London) and an MA in legal and political theory (School of Public Policy, University College London). She has taught sociological theory and methods at City, University of London, the University of Kent and the University of Southampton. Dr Saini is also co-convenor of the British Sociological Association Race and Ethnicity Study Group. Her interests lie in understanding the relationships that middle-class minority ethnic groups in the UK have to their ethnic, religious, national and class identities, and the socio-political implications of this.

Preface

Any book is a social project. It is never simply the sole product of the authors. This book is no exception. It emerges out of a sustained engagement with the British Sociological Association (BSA) and a desire to showcase the importance of the discipline of sociology in the rapidly changing, turbulent and slightly scary contemporary world. This *Short Guide to Sociology* hopes to be the book that we wish we had read years ago. For Rima and Mark, we wish we had known about sociology earlier in our lives so we could have had the language and conceptual framework to make sense of the everyday worlds we grew up in. It is the product of our individual biographies, where we grew up and how we started our careers. We may have grown up in different parts of the UK, and with different backgrounds, but we also grew up in the same social milieu, with similar social forces affecting our life trajectories.

Specifically, this *Short Guide to Sociology* grew out of a project developed with the BSA and Policy Press (which publishes this book). While part of the early career forum of the BSA, Mark edited a booked entitled *Sociologists' Tales* (with Katherine Twamley and Andrea Scott). Conversations continued with the director Alison Shaw and commissioning editor Catherine Gray, who helped to develop the project. The book emerged from a feeling of Mark's that he had had a unique journey into sociology. From talking with others, it was clear that many did not have a conventional route into the discipline. By stimulating the sociological imagination, we realise that we are all unique – just like everyone else.

Being aware that we are not the centre of the universe is humbling. No one individual has the monopoly on how the world works and no individual can claim complete knowledge of the sociological canon.

We all bring different experiences, perspectives and insights to the discipline of sociology. Rima's hard work with the BSA and expertise in teaching provided a broader insight into the undergraduate curriculum to inform the subject matter of this book.

To reiterate that nothing is individual, and everything is social, we would like to thank Alison Shaw and Catherine Gray at Policy Press for their support for this project, alongside the constructive and positive feedback from the reviewers. The BSA is a vital organisation that celebrates the varied and diverse world of sociology and provides the platform for our work to flourish.

Rima would like to thank each of her colleagues and fellow postgraduate students at City, University of London who began her sociological journey with her half a decade ago. Particular thanks go to Aaron Winter, Ipek Demir, Sweta Rajan-Rankin and Narzanin Massoumi, co-convenors of the BSA Race & Ethnicity and Migration study groups, for all the insightful conferences and events they have hosted together, and all the important sociological discussions that have been facilitated by them as a group over the years.

Mark is thankful for being given the opportunity to discover sociology through his PhD supervisor at Exeter, Professor Anthony King. Along the way, he has been supported by many sociologists, too many to mention, who have made him feel like he belonged from his first BSA conference. Special mentions go to Lara Killick and Ruth Lewis who introduce him onto this BSA journey as part of the postgraduate forum.

Clearly, no sociological work would be complete without acknowledging the place of one's family and friends. Mark and Rima's parents and siblings all socialised each of them into this world. Former school friends and work colleagues influenced them and provided the template upon which each sociologist was built. For Rima, by her husband, best friend, and companion through the complexities of this modern world, Amit. For Mark, it has been completed by his partner, best friend and soulmate, Momtaz, to whom he gives eternal thanks.

Mark Doidge and Rima Saini
August 2019

1

Introduction: the sociology of everyday life

It's July 2019 at the time of writing this introduction. The British summer has taken some time to arrive, but the smell of barbeques has started to fill the air. The England football team has just lost in the semi-finals of the World Cup. This is the second tournament in succession that the England team has been defeated at this stage. Their downfall in 2019 followed only a year after the Men's England football team suffered a similar defeat in the semi-final of the Men's World Cup. In contrast, the winners of the 2019 Women's World Cup faced a different battle – after their triumph, no less. Despite their victory, the United States players were locked in a dispute with their national federation over pay. Even though they are more successful on the pitch than their male counterparts, having won the World Cup and Olympic Gold four times apiece, as well as being commercially more successful through shirt sales and corporate endorsements, they were paid substantially less. Added to this, the tournament's star player, Megan Rapinoe, had attracted disdain from the President of the United States because she has been outspoken in terms of equal rights. As well as fighting for equal pay, Rapinoe was the first white player to take a knee in support of the American footballer Colin Kaepernick who led a protest highlighting police violence against African Americans. Rapinoe also highlighted that 'you can't win a championship without gays on your team'. In one brief global tournament, significant social issues like gender inequality, sexuality and racism were all highlighted.

For many people, sport and leisure are everyday occurrences. They structure their friendships, social activities and sense of selves. Through leisure consumption, be it football, music or fashion, friends share video clips, engage in WhatsApp, Snapchat or Instagram conversations, or play games together. Through the social activities of chatting, sharing and doing, young people experiment with their individual identities, curating how they want to be seen to their friends and the world around them. They absorb influences from global fashion companies, advice from older siblings, tips from friends, and ideas from people showcasing their opinions online. Others may disagree with the choices that are made and seek to differentiate themselves, choosing alternative forms of fashion or trying to belittle those that they disagree with. Yet they too will be presenting themselves in a variety of ways to the world around them. And they will do this through the same range of influences: friends, family and social media.

As we try to assert our individual personalities and identities, we draw on a range of traditions, images and ideas. Whether we like grime or K-pop, follow Kylie Jenner or Megan Rapinoe, or play Fortnite or basketball, we build on what came before, listen to what resonates with us, and rebel against what we dislike. Each of these are personal journeys based on where we grew up, who our parents were and what is fashionable at the time. In this maelstrom of influences, sociology helps us to make sense of the world. Understanding individual biographies can help link to those wider social features that influence and shape our lives. It is this link between the individual and society that sociology seeks to understand and explain. It is for this reason that outlining the biographies of the authors can help illustrate both the personal choices they made, and also how those choices were shaped and constrained by external social, economic and political factors.

Mark did not discover sociology; it discovered him. He always felt that he saw the world differently to people around him. Sociology gave him a structure and language to explain this and helped develop his 'sociological eye'. Mark grew up in Devon, but has since moved to Brighton & Hove – two places that could not be more different in how they view the world. Brighton & Hove likes to see itself as a liberal, creative and welcoming city. While Devon is a beautiful place, it has a reputation for being traditional and is very, very white. But listening to Public Enemy, Gil Scott-Heron and political comedy helped him realise that there was a very different world 'out there'. Geographically, the South West is remote from the industrial heartlands of the UK, and from the capital, London. Despite this, it was still historically linked to the industrial development of the UK such as tin mining in Cornwall and shipbuilding in Plymouth. Along the coasts, towns like Torquay, Exmouth and Newquay supplemented their traditional fishing industries with tourism. Workers from the industrial cities would take their vacations at many of the seaside towns across the country. The advent of package holidays to Spain and Greece hit the seaside towns before the de-industrialisation of the UK in the 1980s. Until then, both Labour and Conservative governments subsidised factories to ensure full employment across the country. One such factory was moved to Torbay in the 1950s and Mark's grandfather moved with it, where he worked until he retired. The factory made telecommunications equipment for telephone networks. Both Mark's parents left school and worked in the factory, and that is where they met. His family grew up in a factory house, five minutes' walk from the factory. His dad played snooker at the factory's social club, and most of his childhood was spent with other families who worked at the factory. It just seemed 'normal' and 'sensible' to work there. Not only did Mark go to work there, but so did his two brothers, two cousins and an uncle. Mark was the first member of his family to go to university. He studied law, what he thought was a 'sensible' degree. Needless to say, he didn't enjoy it, but was able to return to work in the factory, a place he had worked during his summer vacations while at university. It felt natural to fall into the traditional heterosexual family model of girlfriend, sensible job and a mortgage. Yet global factors were going to play a part. With the benefit of hindsight, if he had a well-developed sociological imagination then he would have been able to understand what was happening.

The company was a Canadian multinational telecommunications company and had just started to manufacture equipment for the newly developing internet. The dot.com bubble was just starting to inflate when Mark arrived. He was lucky. He worked hard, but the opportunities were there for him to progress. He started off in the warehouse, before becoming warehouse manager, shipping manager and on to various project management jobs. Then the dot.com bubble burst. All the investments started to decrease when the markets realised that there was too much equipment in the system. The factory went through ten rounds of redundancies. His father and uncle were lucky. Due to length of service they received weighty pay offs and pension additions. Others were not so lucky. Eventually the Canadian company was taken over by another company, this time British. They decided to move the manufacturing to China to reduce labour costs. On a personal level, Mark was lucky to experience working in China as he set up the logistics processes and this helped him contemplate a return to university. First through a master's degree in ancient history, then a PhD in sociology. At the height of the dot.com bubble there were 5,000 people working in that factory. Today there are 70. The factory site was derelict for over ten years and is now redeveloped as a retail park. Three generations of many families worked there, but that will no longer be possible. Clearly it had a dramatic impact on his hometown. Lots of people left; there are no jobs. This is not the fault of the individuals there, but global decisions, processes and social changes. Undertaking a sociology degree after being made redundant helped show him that these aren't just personal troubles, but public issues.

Rima grew up in a suburban town straddling Kent and London, one of few children from a minority ethnic background in her local primary and then all-girls grammar school. Her parents, typical of many first generation South Asian families, managed their own small businesses (corner shops and finally a Bed & Breakfast) and, unlike many South Asian immigrants in the 1990s, settled outside of the minority ethnic enclaves in East and West London. They had been part of the latter wave of 'mass migration' from the South Asian subcontinent in the 1970s, both hailing from Punjab in India.

Rima and her sisters 'assimilated' well within their local community, adopting a sense of resilience that, in her current academic research, she finds echoed across many second generation (British born) minority ethnic individuals who seek to not only fit into but to thrive in British society.

As a child Rima was hyper-aware and yet unable to articulate the racial, ethnic and religious differences between herself and her predominantly white British peers. It was only on moving to hugely multicultural Central London for university, by studying international politics specifically, that she learned about colonialism. This was a life-changing historical and ultimately personal insight into race and power that had been overlooked in her standard British school education, where history lessons focused on 20th century Western Europe and little else. She finally understood the longstanding relationship between her country of origin and country of birth, and how the effects of colonialism persist in current global inequalities and structural and everyday racisms. She was also exposed to different sorts of cultures, given the huge swathes of non-UK students who study in London. Not only were her academic horizons opened, but she felt acutely aware, as a young London student, of being a global citizen.

The concept of intersectionality was introduced to Rima as her interests shifted over the years towards sociology. Her parents had told her as a child that she needed to work 'thrice as hard' as others to get ahead, and developing a sociological education allowed her to understand why they believed this was the case, given the pernicious, compounding effects of ethnic and gender biases in the labour market. The changing landscape of social stratification was also something she became somewhat aware of as a teenager but wasn't able to fully understand until her postgraduate sociological education in her mid-twenties. She began to realise how the categories of 'working class' and 'middle class' were not necessarily fit for purpose in representing the sorts of social positioning that a lot of people, particularly someone like herself, a second-generation minority ethnic national with a good education but relatively low economic capital, embodied. Her own academic interests in analysing identities based on class, race and gender developed, and her sociological imagination was ignited.

The sociological imagination

The examples laid out in the opening paragraphs of this introduction provide an excellent starting point to explore what the US sociologist C. Wright Mills (1959) calls 'the sociological imagination'. For Mills, the sociological imagination helps to link 'personal troubles and public issues'. Being made redundant is a personal trouble, but thousands of unemployed people are a public issue. Over the past 30 years there has been a political tendency to individualise personal troubles; unemployment is blamed on individuals, not government policies. Those on welfare are portrayed as lazy, feckless or fraudulent. As the introductory section highlighted, there are many different factors that account for growing inequalities in Britain and how some people have access to the global economy while others are excluded. Whereas we each may have a certain amount of personal choice, or what sociologists call 'agency', there are many structural factors that are outside our personal control.

Sociology allows us to appreciate and understand ourselves through comprehending the wider society around us. By developing a sociological imagination we can make the links between the wider world and our own circumstances and life trajectories. C. Wright Mills said that the key to developing a sociological imagination was through linking personal biography to broader social processes:

> The sociological imagination enables its possessor to understand the larger historical scene in terms of its meaning for the inner life and the external career of a variety of individuals ... The sociological imagination enables us to grasp history and biography and the relations between the two within society ... Perhaps the most fruitful distinction with which the sociological imagination works is between 'the personal troubles of milieu' and 'the public issues of social structure'. (Mills, 1959: 5, 6, 8)

Linking these personal troubles to public issues is one way that developing a sociological imagination can help us to understand our own particular circumstances. But it also helps locate the 'inner life' of how we perceive ourselves with the 'external career' of others and enables us to understand where we sit within those connections.

C. Wright Mills outlined three tendencies of the sociological imagination: history, biography and society. By looking at history, we can see how society can change, and how it is changing. Through people's biographies, we can understand what type of people populate certain social groups and link them to wider networks and organisations. Finally, we need theories that highlight how society is structured and held together. Through our personal biographies, we can see how history has contributed to the employment ups and downs in our hometowns, how they have changed over the years, and how wider factors have affected them. Sociology and the link between personal troubles and public issues (eventually) helped Mark make sense of redundancy and growing up in Devon and Rima understand the differences between herself and those around her.

When C. Wright Mills wrote *The Sociological Imagination* in 1959, he was challenging the established US sociologists of his day to change the world. His challenge still stands today. Not only do we have a duty to engage with the wider world around us, but we should also not be self-absorbed and introspective. Mills argued against sociologists who became overly focused on 'grand theory' and 'abstracted empiricism' without actively engaging with the social world that they studied. He criticised those who developed theories which were supposed to explain everything and also argued against those who went in the opposite direction and produced so much empirical evidence that it became abstracted and removed from any overarching explanation. These writers merely described the social world around them without linking it to any broader understanding or wider theory. Mills argued that sociologists need to combine both theory and empirical data. Those with a sociological imagination need to critically engage with social groups and build an evidence base to argue their case. They also need to critically engage with wider social theories and apply this evidence to prove, disprove or adapt those theories and improve our understanding. Sociology is thus the development of appropriate methods to gather and apply evidence to a suitable social theory.

What is sociology?

Humans are social animals. Whoever we are, we are part of a wide variety of social collectives, from families, schools, religions, classes, castes, jobs, fan groups, friendship groups and gangs. Some of these are broad collectives, such as those based on gender, ethnicity or class; others might be between two people like civil partnerships, marriages or other kinds of intimate relationships. Although we are individuals, we belong to many different social groups and can belong to more than one at any given time. Although the discipline of sociology is the study of society, in reality, it is the study of social groups. Principally, it asks the question of how groups form. Are we free to join any group at will? What role do we play within the group: are we the leader, ideas person or agitator? What rules do we have to play by within the groups and are these rules official or unofficial? Does membership of this group affect how members behave, what they wear, how they interact? As a result, people are judged by which group they belong to, be it a rival football team, a particular profession or a political party.

Sociology is a strange discipline in that everyone – even those without a formal sociological education – can harbour a sociological opinion. The reason for this is that it examines the one thing we all have in common: society. We all see what is important to us and make links between events and feelings. When our towns feel like they are in decline, we look for the causes. It could be corrupt politicians, the EU, immigrants, capitalism or globalisation. When our football team starts losing, we draw connections between the players, manager, owners and rivals. We all develop theories about how things are as they are. This can be about why crime is getting worse (it's rarely about why crime is falling), or how kids are behaving these days. Yet our ways of seeing the world are linked to our upbringing and the context in which we grew up, as well as to diverse global factors.

How we see the world depends on our standpoint. Social media can be a useful medium for keeping in touch with far-flung friends and family, or a source of status anxiety. Heavy metal could be a loud noise, or a great way of drowning out your parents and relaxing in your room. A trip to a Michelin starred restaurant can be the epitome of fine dining, or a pretentious collection of overly elaborate dishes.

Sociology looks beyond these personal standpoints. It seeks to develop clear theories using robust methods of data collection to explore and establish patterns and relationships between new and emerging phenomena in the social world. This moves beyond the confirmation bias of individuals to collect the data that challenges or confirms 'common sense'. If we feel that women drivers are bad drivers, confirmation bias ensures that we only see situations when a female driver has driven badly. Broader statistical analysis of accidents by gender proves otherwise. If we think that people from the rival street, neighbourhood or football team are all stupid idiots, then we start to emphasise the times when they act stupidly. But is this always the case or do they only act in that way when you are around? This 'pub sociology' usually chooses examples to fit the position of the person making the case, rather than developing an argument on the basis of a wide range of evidence explored from different angles.

When sociology confirms 'common sense' it gets dismissed as 'Of course! It's common sense, we always knew that!' When it challenges those everyday assumptions, it gets dismissed as not being about 'the real world'. But sociology specifically sets itself up to tackle these everyday questions. C. Wright Mills said that sociology has to make the familiar strange and the strange familiar. Norbert Elias (1978) said that sociologists were the 'destroyer of myths'. There are many everyday 'myths' that are just accepted as 'common sense' with little underpinning evidence. Sociologists don't blindly follow 'common sense'; we play Devil's advocate and ask contrary questions. We challenge everyday assumptions and received wisdom. Common sense tells us that we should work with 'more haste and less speed', and to 'look before we leap'. Yet it also tells us 'to strike while the iron is hot' and to 'make hay while the sun shines'. Instead of simply assuming that 'the early bird catches the worm', we ask what happens to the worm. Sociologists look at the power relationships within society and ask questions from different perspectives. We listen to a variety of voices and this gives us an overview of society as a whole, not just our small coterie of friends and family.

Sociology is a discipline that requires all the senses. Sociology is a distinctive way of seeing the world. It means developing what the US sociologist Randall Collins (1998) calls a 'sociological eye'. It means being a cynic, searching for hidden meanings behind what is stated. It also entails seeing through the eyes of others, as described by research methods expert Alan Bryman (2012), in order to understand different people's perspectives and interpretations of the world around them. Social life is just the tip of the iceberg and sociologists look for the hidden depths beneath the surface. Analysing everyday activities enables us to think about what is deemed 'common sense', or what is usual and acceptable (what sociologists call 'norms'). The Canadian sociologist Dorothy E. Smith (1987) observed how a simple act of walking her dog revealed the underlying social relations underpinning society. Smith noticed that where she allowed her dog to run or go to the toilet was not a natural journey, but where she felt she would get less judgement from specific homeowners. Even writing this book in a coffee shop reveals a specific set of social relations between baristas, café owners and coffee producers. It also assumes a set of social norms that permit us to sit in a coffee shop and work – sometimes all day – over a single cup of coffee.

Sociology also involves the 'art of listening' as British sociologist Les Back (2007) emphasises. What people say, how and when, are equally as important as what they do. Do their actions match their words? We shall see in Chapter 2 the extent to which our actions are an important part of understanding how people act in society. More importantly, we should let people describe their own experiences and listen empathetically. Feminist, queer and critical race perspectives all centralise the voice and experiences of those who have been marginalised. And let's not forget the other senses: the smells, the tastes, the touches. All of these contribute to a way of understanding the social world around us. And when we develop our 'sociological eye' to see the world around us, and link it to our 'sociological imagination', we will never see the world in the same way again. It opens up a whole host of exciting possibilities, as Randall Collins (1998: 2–3) illustrates:

> There is a sociology of everything. You can turn on your sociological eye no matter where you are or what you are doing. Stuck in a boring committee meeting ... you can check the pattern of who is next to whom, who gets the floor, who makes eye contact, and what is the rhythm of laughter (forced or spontaneous) or of pompous speechmaking. Walking down the street, or out for a run, you can scan the class and ethnic pattern of the neighbourhood, look for the lines of age segregation, or for little pockets of solidarity. Waiting for a medical appointment, you can read the professions and the bureaucracy instead of the old copies of *National Geographic*. Caught in a traffic jam, you can study the correlation of car models with bumper stickers or with the types of music blaring from radios. There is literally nothing you can't see in a fresh way if you turn your sociological eye to it. Being a sociologist means never having to be bored.

While every discipline has its own way of seeing the world, sociology helps us see the everyday in new and exciting ways. Sociologists seem almost unique in getting excited about the everyday and challenging 'common sense' assumptions.

Many people come to sociology because they are interested in social inequalities. This also sets the discipline apart from others. Sociologists care acutely about the world around them. C. Wright Mills argued that sociology had a duty to feed back into the social world around us and improve it. US sociologist Howard Becker asked sociologists 'whose side are we on?' It is impossible for sociologists to undertake research 'uncontaminated by personal and political sympathies' (Becker, 1967: 240). Few people criticise those whose findings confirm the position of those in power. Criticism only emerges when dominant ideas, theories or discourses are challenged. What makes sociologists distinctive is that we acknowledge this and reflect on our own position and practice. Alvin Gouldner (1968) argues that it is not simply about choosing sides, but that we have a duty to present the story from all perspectives; no single perspective should be privileged. This is vital as 'it gives us new information concerning social worlds about which many members of our society, including ourselves, know little or nothing' (Gouldner, 1968: 105). Many sociologists care passionately about presenting the voice of the voiceless. For Randall Collins (1998: 4), 'sociology has two core commitments: ... the "sociological eye" and social activism'. It is for this reason that this book and many others like it seek to showcase the experiences and voices of women, those belonging to minority ethnic groups, non-heterosexual sexualities and non-elite social classes. This is not to celebrate or promote certain groups, but to help us understand the wider perspective. By understanding and analysing the stories of people who are different from us, we learn more about ourselves and society as a whole.

Sociology is thus an emotional discipline. Sociologists care about the social world and can empathise with the various groups that we study. We don't pathologise problems and claim that they are solely the fault of the individual or their personal nature. We analyse a variety of factors and come to a balanced and informed view. 'It helps us', as Gouldner (1968: 105) points out, 'to do the distinctive job we have' – to challenge 'common sense' and ultimately improve the world around us.

Outline of the book

By developing our sociological imagination and linking personal troubles to public issues, we can understand the impact of globalisation on local communities and individuals. This book will outline two broad impacts: cultural and economic. The cultural effects are varied and affect social demographics differently. These relate to food, music, sport, entertainment and other types of leisure consumption. Some of these impact on how we understand others and relate to our friendships, sexualities and relationships. The economic effects, as outlined above, are on things like the types of jobs available, the skills required to fill them – whether from domestic or immigrant labour – their pay and conditions, and the inequalities that result.

This book will account for these changes by taking the reader on a journey through everyday life. It will address changing identities and highlight how these are reflected in our leisure consumption and relationships, and how these are embedded within broader issues around class, race and gender. In particular, the book will demonstrate how these various aspects of our identities, lifestyle and consumption have changed, but also how inequality remains. Finally, it presents this against the backdrop of 'Brexit', de-industrialisation and globalisation with all the social and political tensions and structural changes these are bringing. Broadly, the book presents two expansive phases in primarily British post-war society.

After the Second World War there was a fairly stable social world based on state-controlled economies and fairly rigid social roles. The family ideal was based on the nuclear family of a heterosexual union between a husband and wife based on the male breadwinner and female housewife and carer of the family. While women had the right to vote on the same terms as men by 1928, females were still considered 'the second sex', the inferior gender. Male homosexuality was illegal and forced out of the public gaze. Even though the UK was an imperial power with a long history of global migration, racism began to emerge as families from former colonies in the West Indies, Africa, South Asia and Hong Kong established themselves in the UK. Class was also based around the industrial working class, middles classes of managers and professionals, and the old landed aristocratic class. At the end of the 1960s there was a flurry of social legislation that liberalised many social practices, notably the Race Relations Act (1965), the Sexual Offences Act (1967), the Divorce Reform Act (1969), and the Sex Discrimination Act (1975). Alongside this began the sexual revolution, partially thanks to the invention of the contraceptive pill, which gave women more choice over reproduction. New identities around consumption grew at the same time as fashion and music took a central role in people's lives. Various social movements, particularly with regard to women's liberation, gay rights, civil rights, anti-war and the environment, also emerged to challenge the existing political and social order.

Economic liberalisation followed in the 1970s and more swiftly in the 1980s. Governments led by Margaret Thatcher and Ronald Reagan, in the UK and US respectively, undertook a process of economic deregulation that focused on shrinking the role of the state. National industries were privatised, state subsidies were removed and regulations controlling commerce were loosened. Many of the UK's industries closed down and moved to countries with cheaper labour, such as China. The economy restructured around services such as finance, research and development, and the creative industries. All of these required higher qualifications and most were based around London and, to a lesser extent, Manchester. The UK became a post-industrial nation and its society became polarised around the global cities and the former industrial towns and cities. All of this was facilitated by technology such as cheap and easy air travel and the internet, which allow us to communicate with ease with pretty much anyone in the world. Our society became more globalised in a matter of years as time and space compressed.

Ultimately this book makes three important points. First, many voices in the media, politics and academia talk of a social breakdown: old social forms are disintegrating, community is crumbling and we are heading to social Armageddon. Some academics will talk of society becoming 'individualised'. While it is true that the social and economic changes of the 1970s and 1980s have had a profound impact on the social world around us, we are not hyper-autonomous beings that act independently of everyone else. Our friends, family, lovers, communities, political beliefs, lifestyle choices and more still profoundly influence us, potentially more so now in times of political instability. Think about your own world and really question whether you are an isolated individual. It is unlikely that if you are reading this book that you are a hermit living in solitude on some desert island. How you dress, act and think are all influenced by the people and society around you. While we may be more aware of a sense of individuality, and consumer capitalism and legal freedoms allow us to explore this, we are still linked to any number of groups, friends, family and movements. These have just changed in form and purpose since the 1960s.

Second, despite political arguments to the contrary, social inequalities continue. While there has been a dramatic social transformation over the last 40 years, discrimination and inequality persist. The removal of legal barriers around gender, ethnicity and sexuality, as well as economic liberalisation, may have opened up opportunities for some social mobility, but this has not created a more equal or meritocratic society. Far from it. Those who have the right social attributes (cultural capital) or personal connections (social capital) are still privileged in the workplace, which brings its own economic rewards. Principally, this is still white, heterosexual men with the 'right' education and connections. Explicit discrimination may have declined, but a much more subtle form of discrimination has replaced it. Women and those of minority ethnicity are still more likely to earn much less than their white and male counterparts. Gendered divisions continue within the home and in our relationships. And certain ethnic groups are still targeted as outsiders by sections of the media, politicians and society. Young black men continue to be the target of excessive police attention, while young white and minority ethnic men are excluded from sections of the job market through educational disadvantage.

Third, there is a paradox of sociology. We cannot understand ourselves as individuals until we understand the wider social world. After starting his sociological career, Mark discovered where he belonged in society. He understood why his family had all worked in the same place, why he settled for a 'conventional' life, and perhaps why so many people settle for the easy life. Rima understood more acutely why her parents had moved to build a sensible life, and the struggles they had in doing so. By knowing their place in society, they would have been able to better understand how to navigate their way through. They would have understood the importance of networks – it's not what you know but who you know. Sociology taught Rima and Mark about the importance of knowing the right people. It taught them about exclusion, particularly for women and those from minority ethnic groups, but also about how economics excludes those without the skills to access the changing economy.

This book does not intend to be the definitive guide to sociology. We do not claim to be experts in all of the topics written about and we should acknowledge our own privilege in being able to write this book. You do not have to agree with everything that we have written. The intention is that this should whet your appetite for seeing the world through a sociological eye. There is a wealth of sociological literature to analyse even the most mundane of activities. We touch on some of the 'bigger' topics within these pages, but it is possible to develop a sociological imagination about everything and anything. Human beings are an infinitely interesting, changing and challenging group of creatures. Even through everyday activities like food, music, sport, sex, clothes and religion, we can see how humans have changed over time and how they differ across the world today.

A not-so-secret hope of this book is that the reader will critically engage with the world. Being a sociologist is like being the child in Hans Christian Andersen's fable of the Emperor's New Clothes (Twamley et al, 2015). It is a useful metaphor for sociology. Often sociologists are the ones pointing out the problems of everyday life. Many people accede to those with power and refuse to challenge the status quo. Yet as soon as we pierce the hypocrisy of those in power, then everyone says 'of course' it's obvious – sociology is just telling us what we already know.

Ultimately, sociology helps us to understand the big questions like populism, globalisation and migration. It does not provide a simple answer, but highlights the complexity of life. It provides a critical voice that challenges those in power and emphasises that their invisible threads of power can be unwoven quickly. Sociology enables us to locate ourselves as individuals within the grand scheme of things and helps us to understand our own identities, genders, sexualities, social status and personal relationships. Ultimately, sociology provides us with a range of skills and tools that enable us to navigate through the world. By developing a critical 'sociological eye' to observe the world and building a 'sociological imagination' to link the various aspects of personal biographies, history and society together, then we can see the world more clearly. It is fair to say that once you see the world sociologically, you will never see it in the same way again.

2

Lifestyle and consumption

When Stormzy walked out onto the Glastonbury stage in the summer's evening of June 2019, he made several important political statements. On a basic level, Stormzy announced the commercial arrival of grime music at a festival that has usually headlined rock bands in its 50-year history. Being the first black British male to headline the world-famous Pyramid stage, however, could have indicated that the UK's multicultural population was finally getting acceptance. Yet his attire suggested the opposite. Stormzy wore a stab vest (designed by the artist Banksy) to highlight the disproportionate number of young black men criminalised in the British criminal justice system. Alongside Stormzy, the black and minority ethnic (BME) dance group Ballet Black danced, highlighting the lack of diversity in the high cultural art forms of ballet and opera. This wasn't the first time that grime artists had made political statements. Three years earlier, Stormzy, Akala and others united under #Grime4Corbyn to endorse party politics and, more specifically, the Labour Party leader Jeremy Corbyn as the next prime minister. While Skepta has since argued that mainstream politicians and media cynically exploited this movement, it highlighted a significant moment when a youth subculture became explicitly linked to the broader politics of the country; a journey that continued with Stormzy headlining Glastonbury.

This chapter will show how lifestyle and consumption choices, like grime or football, have changed over the past 50 years. These reflect the wider social, economic and political changes that have taken place. They also help explain some of the demographic differences between age groups in the UK. Often these youth identities perplex older generations and this results in a cycle of 'moral panics' that demonise young people. Frequently the media label an entire generation and employ pub sociology to seek to identify similarities between members and how they are different from other generations. Frequently these 'groups' are associated with troubling behaviour as the media seek to highlight how the youth of today are inferior to those of the past. As well as grime and drill music, the contemporary focus is on millennials or the 'snowflake generation' (see Box 2.1). Frequently written by older white men, these accounts suggest that this generation is emotionally and psychologically weak compared to the resilient generations of the past.

Box 2.1: Millennials and snowflakes: how do we differentiate between generations in today's society?

Millennials constitute a broad group in society, generally referring to those born between 1980 and 2000 –the first generation to come of age in the new millennium. This is a broad group, however, given the technological changes occurring during these decades. Latter millennials or 'Generation Z' were raised on smartphones, apps and tablets, which came about in the 2000s. In popular culture, they are often referred to pejoratively, as 'snowflakes'. It is a term that suggests young people have an overinflated sense of their own uniqueness, just as the snowflake is unique. The implication is that these unique individuals are highly sensitive to causes that affect them and have lower resilience. However, they have also been seen as victims of austerity politics and rising house prices, which have seen low job and house creation, a rising cost of living and a shrinking welfare state.

Taking a sociological lens to these accounts will help to explain the broader picture. Rather than dismissing an entire generation, sociologists link broader social issues to individual biographies. As this book shows, there have been significant changes to British society over the past 40 years. How we see ourselves as individuals, and how we see race, gender, class and sexuality have all changed. Older generations have helped enact these changes, but don't always agree with the pace or pattern of change. Younger generations embody these changes and, consequently, highlight the previous generation's fears.

In this chapter we will notice a similar pattern to other chapters within this book. Social life and social identities used to be tied to locality and nation, and particularly around work. By the mid-1960s global influences, mainly from the US, but also from Europe and the former British Empire, influenced our lifestyle choices, our music and our subcultures. By the 1980s these lifestyles became more flexible. Today we have more fluid approaches to consumption and fewer distinct subcultures. A similar pattern can be observed with sport. Team sports were followed by people from the immediate locality. There was a more rigid class, race and gender structure that governed who could play and watch these sports. By the 1970s we start to see a more global and commercial development in sport, led by FIFA, the international football federation, and followed by the International Olympic Committee (IOC). By the late 1980s businesses were more involved in sport, and football in particular, and saw it as a business investment, rather than people's identity. Yet the growth of sport also fed into other lifestyles. Sports clothing is now ubiquitous on the high street, and some sports, such as surfing and skateboarding, explicitly combine fashion and sport.

Technology has dramatically impacted how we consume. Developments in lean manufacturing (which will be looked at in Chapter 7) have improved high street fashion retailers' access to cheaper supply chains and distribution to customers. This gives consumers more choice of a variety of fashions and styles and they can experiment with their image and how they choose to present themselves. Traditional and social media also provide a wider window to a variety of images and styles from around the world. The British sociologist Anthony Giddens said that globalisation was 'time-space compression'. The internet doesn't just allow us to share present information across the world; it also allows us to see into the past. We can hear music from across the world and incorporate it into our identity. But we can also access music from 50 years ago. We are no longer reliant on the local record store having the record or CD in stock; we can download or stream the track immediately.

Our lifestyles and how we consume provide powerful symbols for our society. They simultaneously represent our identities and how we choose to present ourselves, and reflect the changing political and economic environment around us. Yet they also become 'normalised' and seen as 'natural' and 'common sense'. In *Mythologies* (1957), the highly influential French cultural theorist Roland Barthes deconstructs these 'myths' and shows how these images are appropriated by dominant social culture and presented as 'natural' and taken for granted. Barthes used the powerful symbol of the young black soldier saluting an unseen French flag on a magazine cover to highlight how this act of loyalty (the salute) also symbolises that 'France is a great empire, and all her sons, without colour discrimination, faithfully serve under her flag' (Barthes, 1957). More importantly, it denotes that the nation is 'natural' and 'normal'. Like our identities they are represented through regular performance and over time this becomes seen as 'natural' or 'normal'. Yet our sociological imagination permits us to see how these symbols change over time, and to look at the power dynamics that operate.

Subcultures, music and fashion

Whether it's Chavs or hip hop, video games or skateboarding, since the Second World War, young people have been seen as both the creative force of change and the fearful moral decline of the UK. Growing affluence after the Second World War saw the emergence of the social category of the teenager. These young people no longer had to work in order to support the family and this free time and more disposable income found an outlet in certain forms of consumption, particularly music and fashion. From Teddy Boys to mods and rockers, through hippies and punks to goths and grime, youth subcultures are expressive ways of developing individual identity and distinction from parents and other groups. Through consumption, young people in particular can explore their own identities and develop a distinctive sense of self.

As will be explored in Chapter 7, the economies in Western Europe and North America were organised around policies that promoted full employment underpinned by mass manufacturing. This ensured that there were higher wages and more consumer goods to purchase. While suburban families bought cars, televisions and washing machines, young people were able to buy their own clothes to clearly differentiate themselves from their parents. Mandatory education also ensured that young people stayed in school for longer rather than starting work. Not only were they gaining an education, they were also allowed some space to develop their own independent identities. Money and time enabled them to do this. All of this allowed the teenager to become a social being.

Post-war youth subcultures highlight a growing global influence (Hall and Jefferson, 1976; Hebdige, 1979). Early influences came from the US, then France and Italy, and latterly through migration from former colonies in the British Empire. Through underground magazines, movies and 'moral panics' in the traditional media, members could learn about new identities. Beatniks emerged in the late 1940s in New York and incorporated a style of dress (a turtleneck jumper, beret), goatee beards (for the men), smoking French cigarettes or marijuana, listening to bebop jazz and discussing French existential philosophy. A more popular subculture in the UK was the Teddy Boys. This predominately masculine subculture wore Edwardian-style suits that were similar to zoot suits worn by African Americans and Italian Americans. Their hair was styled into a quiff and modelled on the US movie star Tony Curtis. Teddy Girls wore similar jackets with pencil skirts. Rock and roll and skiffle were the predominant musical choices – both from the US. These styles marked a dramatic difference from their parents' clothing and musical style and were a marked contrast to the more austere times of post-war Britain.

Subcultures in the 1960s and 1970s saw a similar US provenance, with some European and West Indian influences, particularly through the styles and music from new migrants from the West Indies. The mods and rockers were two groups that highlighted the subcultural divide and the different influence from the US and Europe. Rockers grew out of the Teddy Boys. They were listening to rock music and influenced by US movies such as *A Streetcar Named Desire* and *Rebel Without A Cause*. While mass produced cars were affordable to middle-class families, they were out of reach to young people. The boom in industrial production also boosted the manufacture of motorbikes that could be bought on credit. In contrast, mods rode Italian scooters like Vespas and Lambrettas, which were also the result of an economic miracle in Italy. Scooters allowed mods to dress in smart suits or dresses that were influenced by French and Italian films like *La Dolce Vita*. This style of dress differentiated from the leather and jeans of rockers, who, as their name suggests, listened to rock music. For mods, US influence came in the shape of the black music of jazz and rhythm and blues, while others listened to ska, brought to the UK by Jamaican immigrants. This style became the core of the Swinging Sixties image of the UK before being incorporated into the growing hippy movement from the US.

By the late 1970s youth subcultures were reflecting the discordant social world around them. The punk scene sought to radically differentiate itself from previous subcultures and the social world around them with dramatically different hairstyles that were dyed, spiked or cut into mohawks. Ripped jeans, leather jackets and boots were worn by both men and women. All of this was associated with punk music that grew up in London and New York. At the same time in the UK there was a mod revival movement linked to bands like *The Jam* and the skinhead revival movement that was originally associated with Jamaican ska in the 1960s, before becoming more political in the early 1980s and associated with extreme right and left wing politics. Black music from the US and the West Indies began to assert itself on British subcultures in the 1970s. Club culture emerged from the soul and funk that grew out of rhythm and blues. This diverged into disco and the roots of club culture in the 1980s and 1990s, while the beats and rhymes also spawned rap and hip hop. Club culture and sportswear were the key ingredients of the 'casuals', who were football fans who travelled around Europe supporting their team and adopting Italian and French fashion sportswear brands like Fila, Ellesse and Lacoste. Casuals became associated with hooliganism and reflected the growing link the establishment would make between subcultures and deviance.

Box 2.2: Identity: what makes us who we are?

An individual's set of personal and collective identities are not distinct and separate; they are entangled and intersecting. In some cases we become more aware of certain parts of our identities when we are placed in situations where we are aware of our difference. Paradoxically we may be more aware of our Britishness when we live abroad. Likewise, we may become aware of our skin colour when we are in an environment where our skin colour is in the minority. Being confronted with difference helps us determine who 'we' are.

Identity is not just about difference. In order to know who 'we' are, we also need to know what similarities we have. What makes us Scottish rather than British? How are we British, rather than European? Why is someone Afro-Caribbean, rather than Bajan, British, or Cockney? Why does one have to be female, rather than an accountant or a charity worker? For many of these identities, it is about what links us to other people. In some senses, it is linked to broader and often minoritised identities like gender, class and race. Others are linked to our forms of consumption, like what music we listen to, which football team we support or the type of clothes we wear. Through interacting with others, we reflect back on ourselves and adjust our behaviours according to how we wish to be seen (Mead, 1934).

We all undertake what US sociologist Erving Goffman (1959) calls 'impression management'. In *The Presentation of Self in Everyday Life*, Goffman (1959) suggests that we choose different roles based on the audience we are facing. We prepare for these roles backstage, before undertaking the performance. This can involve choosing the right clothes, putting on makeup, or making sure we say or do the right things. These roles are more obvious in situations such as interviews, when working in the service sector or meeting new people. But they also operate when we are relaxed and with friends and family. Looking through photos on social media is a journey through Goffman's 'presentation of self'. Some of these will be on nights out which show how sociable we are, or with our boyfriend or girlfriend to tell others that we are in a relationship, or to communicate our social and political stances.

These subcultures incorporated music, fashion, new social behaviours and activities, like drug-taking or violence, that upset the older, established generation (which will be discussed in more detail later). Often subcultures would seek to establish clear boundaries from other groups. As Jamaican-British cultural studies pioneer Stuart Hall (1996: 4) highlighted, one's identity is through exclusion and difference:

> [Identities] emerge within the play of specific modalities of power, and thus are more the product of the marking of difference and exclusion, than they are the sign of an identical, naturally-constituted unity ... Above all, and directly contrary to the form in which they are constantly invoked, identities are constructed through, not outside, difference ... identities can function as points of identification and attachment only because of their capacity to exclude, to leave out, to render 'outside'.

For Stuart Hall, being an outsider is about power and excluding people who don't conform to the dominant group's values, ideas or behaviours. In *Outsiders* (1963), US sociologist Howard Becker observed how members of the so-called deviant groups would establish their own boundaries and rules in order to differentiate themselves from others. Becker noted that jazz musicians would reinforce how they were more authentic and knowledgeable than the people paying to listen to their music. In this way, social groups reinforce their own boundaries and differentiate themselves from others. This is also done through key cultural symbols, like forms of dress, Vespas or motorbikes, hairstyle or music.

Subcultures are simultaneously seen as resisting the dominant culture and being incorporated into that dominant culture. We return to Roland Barthes and his 'myths' in that subcultures contain a range of symbols that can be analysed, such as long or short hair, Vespas or Triumphs, or Ben Sherman or Adidas. But they also highlight a relationship with dominant culture. In *Resistance Through Rituals* (Hall and Jefferson, 1976), various authors highlight how subcultures are a working-class resistance against bourgeois culture. Through consumption, members of youth subcultures, like mods and rockers, punks and Rastafarians, are differentiating themselves from other subcultures and the dominant culture.

Capitalism finds a way to commodify and sell the images and symbols of subculture to a mass market. In *Subculture: The Meaning of Style* (1979), British sociologist Dick Hebdige highlights how subcultures are a way of 'dramatising' the broader cultural environment. Style is a form of performance. Members are communicating their identity through their clothing and hairstyles. Yet this also draws wider attention from established society.

In most cases, it is the subculture's stylistic innovations that first attract the media's attention. Subsequently deviant or 'antisocial' acts – vandalism, swearing, fighting, 'animal behaviour' – are 'discovered' by the police, the judiciary and the press; these acts are used to 'explain' the subculture's original transgression of sartorial codes (Hebdige, 1979: 93).

Very quickly, however, the subculture becomes appropriated by the wider consumer society. 'Each new subculture,' Hebdige (1979: 95) argues, 'establishes new trends, generates new looks and sounds which feed back into the appropriate industries.' Stormzy headlining Glastonbury shows how a musical form criticised by the mainstream suddenly becomes headline material.

Despite the quick commercial appropriation, different forms of dress can also create anxiety among others who see a visible change in culture. For those outside the subculture, different styles of dress symbolise a challenge to their culture and way of life. This can be seen in concern over groups like Teddy Boys and punks, or items of clothing like hoodies or hijabs. Often these lead to 'moral panics' and media stories about the declining morality of youth and the dangerous influence of certain forms of music, video games or other leisure activities. The term 'moral panic' was coined by British criminologist Stanley Cohen in *Folk Devils and Moral Panics* (1972). He analysed the approach of the media presentation of fights between mods and rockers in British seaside towns in the early 1960s and identified how youth subcultures are described in moral terms about the declining morality of the nation. Cohen observed how the media present a 'folk devil' that draws on the subculture's image, while their identity is oversimplified to present a clear narrative. Deviant acts that are undertaken by a group that fit this image are exaggerated and the media embark on a 'moral crusade' to prevent future events from happening. These media stories do two things: they draw more police, political and media attention to the groups, and they simultaneously attract more people to the subculture. This 'justifies' the moral condemnation and political attention. Eventually these moral panics subside as a new group becomes the focus.

Moral panics often suggest a 'golden age' where society and morality were stronger. Our sociological imagination can link this stability to a different political and economic climate. Not only does nostalgia for a 'golden age' ignore the concerns that existed around Teddy Boys, mods and rockers, hippies and punks, it also shows how moral panics repeat. The British criminologist Geoffrey Pearson observed in *Hooligan: A History of Respectable Fears* (1983) that during the Second World War there were concerns about Blitz kids engaged in crime. Before that, there was a moral panic around Hollywood movies leading to an increase in crime. These patterns went back into the 19th century, where hooligans were young street urchins engaged in crime and fighting. And we can see how the pattern of moral panics continues, from hooligans to Acid House, from single mothers to Islamic groups, from hip hop to video games. These groups are almost always working class, usually male and more frequently non-white. For Pearson and Cohen, moral panics are ways in which the dominant social group exerts its control.

Subcultures reflect the patterns of consumption in wider society. As shown in Box 2.2, identities are not fixed and adapt to different contexts. Writers on subcultures overwhelmingly focused on male (McRobbie and Garber, 1976) and working-class subcultures (Bennett and Kahn-Harris, 2004). Because of this they failed to see the changing consumption patterns associated with these forms of identities. While we can still observe certain distinct subcultures like goths (Hodkinson, 2002), in *Club Cultures*, Canadian sociologist Sarah Thornton argues that these subcultures are less rigid and are seen as 'ad hoc communities with fluid boundaries' (Thornton, 1995: 3). And this links to what French sociologist Michel Maffesoli argued when he challenged the arguments suggesting that society is becoming more individualised by suggesting that new 'tribes' were forming. These are, according to Maffesoli (1996: 98), 'without the rigidity of the forms of organisation with which we are familiar, it refers to a certain ambience, a state of mind, and is preferably to be expressed through lifestyles that favour appearance and form'. Lifestyles are expressed through various forms of consumption and these vary depending on whom our audience is and how we are feeling. We can be a football fan on a Saturday afternoon, but a punk in the evening. We can be an architect during the week, but a surfer on the weekends.

Academic interest in subcultures often focused on lifestyles that were predominantly white, from mods and rockers, punks, to goths and club culture. As the opening paragraph to this chapter outlined, young black subcultures are often stigmatised as gangs and inciting violence. Dick Hebdige highlighted in *Resistance Through Rituals* (1976) that the growth of Rastafarianism in the UK in the 1960s and 1970s was a cultural resistance to dominant racist white culture at the time. It was a way of asserting a racialised social identity tied to race, place and culture. Like soul and jazz music from the US, reggae has its roots in slaves taken from West Africa. This music emphasises the rhythm, with certain lyrical flourishes, often call and responses, and poetic rhymes of the rhythm. Like hip hop before them, grime and drill music acted as a racialised form of identity. And as with previous subcultures, these identities were often viewed with suspicion, or worse, criminalised. Despite this, black cultural influences have been incorporated into wider popular music, from jazz and blues forming the foundation of rock, to hip hop and RnB dominating contemporary music scenes. Culture and subculture are not fixed or essentialised, but adapt over time.

Sport

Alongside music and fashion, sport represents a major part of many people's everyday lives. Even those that don't like sport often have to express that they don't like sport. As a regular physical practice, sport provides a key part of many people's identity. For many it is an opportunity to assert their individuality and independence from family. For others it provides a sense of place through their locality or their nation. Sportswear has become everyday clothing for many people across the world. Sport also provides another useful case study of globalisation and the changes in contemporary society. Historically sport was something done locally, predominantly by men and often by the middle classes who had the resources to take part. Sport is important as it became more central in people's lives during the 19th century when workers in the cities started winning more free time from their employers. Political and religious leaders were concerned about the morality of the working classes (there's a theme here!) and felt that sport would be a good way to keep them out of the pubs and gambling dens. Sport, and football in particular, gave people a connection to their new city and helped generate feelings of belonging.

Football fandom is an everyday activity for many people. It is an easy conversation starter for strangers (particularly men), and structures regular meetings between friends and acquaintances as they congregate to watch matches at the stadium, at home or in the pub. For many, the football club becomes an extension of themselves as they say 'we won on Saturday' or 'I can't wait until the weekend as we are playing United'. The team's successes and failures become symbolic of the individual, as well as the city. When Leicester City won the Premier League title in 2016, this was a celebration for the whole city, not just those fans who went every week. England's relative success at the 2015 and 2019 World Cups were indicative of the status of women's football. In some cases, the clubs become symbolic of wider social identities, such as Protestants and Catholics in Glasgow with Rangers and Celtic. The 'other', as Stuart Hall highlighted earlier, sharpens these identities. Football fandom is an excellent way of understanding how individual identities are connected to wider social collectives or who *we* are, compared to who *they* are.

International competition in sports also helps to sharpen national identity. International competition provides a symbolic space for nations to showcase themselves to the world. When the Olympic Games began in 1896, their founder, French aristocrat Pierre de Coubertin, expressly wanted to provide an opportunity for nations to compete without resorting to war. This demonstrates how the politics of nationalism is a 'common sense' that rarely gets questioned during sporting competitions. Yet these sporting events also provide opportunities for former colonies to establish their own national histories as well as defeating their former colonial overlords. The great Trinidadian scholar C.L.R. James (1963: 225) outlines the social importance of sport in developing a wider consciousness:

What do they know of cricket who only cricket know? West Indians crowding to Tests bring with them the whole past history and future hopes of the islands. English people, for example, have a conception of themselves breathed from birth. Drake and mighty Nelson, Shakespeare, Waterloo, the Charge of the Light Brigade, the few who did so much for so many, the success of parliamentary democracy, those and such as those constitute a national tradition. Underdeveloped countries have to go back centuries to rebuild one. We of the West Indies have none at all, none that we know of. To such people the three W's, Ram and Val wrecking English batting, help to fill a huge gap in their consciousness and in their needs. (James, 1963: 225)

Sport provides opportunities for fans, players, clubs and nations to construct their narratives and traditions and showcase themselves to the world. It is for this reason that nations and cities make ever larger investments to host global events, despite there being no clear evidence that they financially benefit the city or nation (Horne and Whannel, 2012).

The London 2012 Olympic and Paralympic Games were held in an attempt to sell the UK and London. The Games represent a paradox: they are hosted by cities but competed between nations. The opening ceremony was a mixture of national and London-oriented symbols. The ceremony highlighted the contribution the UK made to the world, from the industrial revolution through the cultural revolution of the 1960s to the internet revolution in the late 20th century. These neatly highlight the broad social changes that have taken place nationally and globally, as outlined throughout this book. There was celebration of the NHS and British music from the Swinging Sixties onwards, including ska, punk, grime and bhangra. It culminated with a digitally connected globe, thanks to internet pioneer Sir Tim Berners-Lee, declaring 'this is for the world'. While this clearly outlined the UK's role in the world, it also highlighted that we were now in a digital age and connected globally.

London was also sold through the opening ceremony. This was clear in the James Bond sequence that introduced the Queen to the stadium. While the Queen and James Bond are symbols of Britain, and the film included the Union Flag, the rest of the sequence was designed to showcase London. The helicopter transporting 007 and the British monarch to the Olympic Stadium flew over key London landmarks, including Buckingham Palace, the Houses of Parliament, the London Eye, St Paul's Cathedral and Tower Bridge. More importantly, it flew over the city of London where a group of bankers celebrated with champagne. The message was clear; London was a city of investment. London was also sold through the use of iconic locations for sporting events. Alongside the Olympic Stadium, events were held at Wimbledon, Wembley and Lords to tell the world that London was the sporting capital of the world. Events were also held in Horseguards Parade, Hyde Park, Greenwich Park, Earls Court and the O2 arena to show the pleasant surroundings and opportunities to be found in London. The use of the London Marathon course for the marathon simply underlined both aspects.

London 2012 also illustrated Britain's growing multiculturalism. The successful Team GB was comprised of many different ethnicities, ages and genders, as were the widely praised volunteers. One of the stars of the Games was Mo Farah, who won golds in both the 5,000 and 10,000 metre races. Farah came from a family of Somali refugees who had fled the East African country in the late 1980s. Despite Farah's success, world titles and gold medals, this has not stopped certain journalists questioning if he is 'truly British'. As the British sociologist Ben Carrington (2010: 4) argues, 'it is sports assumed innocence as a space and place that is removed from concerns of power, inequality, struggle and ideology, that has, paradoxically, allowed it to be filled with a range of contradictory assumptions that have inevitably spilled back over and into wider society'. Sport is not ideologically neutral. The *Daily Mail* ran a campaign against 'plastic Brits' who were born outside the UK and still allowed to compete for Team GB.[1] It is no surprise that the athletes targeted in this campaign were all black, which challenged certain people's conceptions of 'Britishness'. In contrast, there was no scrutiny of the cyclists Bradley Wiggins, who was born in Belgium with an Australian father, and Kenyan-born Chris Froome. Their whiteness didn't lead them to be questioned over their right to compete for Team GB.

Everyday identity is exhibited in sport through fashion. When US rappers Run DMC released *My Adidas* in 1986, they not only showcased the importance of the sportswear brand in hip hop culture but also how young people wearing sportswear were unfairly targeted as troublemakers. Yet Adidas had already had a considerable commercial impact on sport which helped to propel it into the minds of urban subcultures in the US and UK. Adolph 'Adi' Dassler, the founder of Adidas (from the portmanteau of his name: Adi Das) began making running shoes in 1924 in Western Germany, near the French border. From the 1940s, he used the three stripes of leather that held the shoe together as a distinguishing feature in order to differentiate his product from others. At this time, he fell out with his brother, Rudolph, who set up a rival sportswear company called Puma. Rudolph also chose a distinctive brand for his shoes, but focused on football boots, whereas Adidas was mainly running shoes. Adi Dassler's son Horst took this one stage further. From 1974, Horst Dassler worked with the president of FIFA, the Brazilian João Havelange, to increase the global reach of football and expand the market for Adidas. With his business partner Patrick Nally, Dassler suggested that FIFA should restrict sponsorship of the World Cup to a small number of sponsors. These companies should be international in order to work in a global market (Sugden and Tomlinson, 1999). The 1970s coincided with the growth of transnational corporations who were looking to expand globally. Nally and Dassler approached Pepsi and Coca Cola with the exclusive rights to the World Cup. Pepsi failed to respond and Coca Cola agreed. With the world's most recognisable brand, and Adidas of course, FIFA was able to approach other global corporations. The key was not to have brands in the same market, but different markets. The result was a range of corporate partners from the fields of soft drinks, telecommunications, electrical equipment, finance, and so on. This approach restricted the rights of the FIFA brand, which increased the amount they could request for its use. The IOC introduced this with The Olympic Program in 1984 and has been widely copied by football leagues, and other world cups.

Media, and television in particular, are also important for the promotion of sport (and, by extension, the corporate partners like Coca Cola). As Sarah Thornton (1995) mentions in relation to music and subculture, the media is central in promoting an image. In sport, this has been achieved by restricting access to sporting events. Until the 1970s sport was seen as another news event, so television costs were low. But with the increase of television ownership thanks to post-war affluence, television companies wanted to compete for audience share. Horst Dassler set up a media company called International Sport and Leisure and obtained the exclusive television rights from FIFA (and subsequently from the IOC) before selling them on to select television companies. A golden triangle formed between corporate sponsors, television and sport that ensured they each promoted each other.

Despite the success of the Olympics, the Games also have to adapt to changing identities and lifestyles. Certain sports that have been in the Olympics since 1896 are no longer television friendly. Other sporting tournaments have taken off in the past 30 years to appeal to a younger audience that has grown disillusioned with traditional sports. Lifestyle sports like surfing, skateboarding, mountain biking and snowboarding have all blurred the boundaries between sport and lifestyle (Wheaton 2004). These leisure activities are not necessarily about competition but about an associated lifestyle. They have grown in parallel with specific businesses that help promote and sell the lifestyle associated with the sport. Brands like Quiksilver, Rip Curl, Vans and Burton have all grown out of these sporting activities. Other brands, in particular Red Bull, actively promote their product by aligning to lifestyle sport events. Specialised media, in particular videos and magazines, helped to publicise and promote these activities around the world. Other urban activities like parkour have also developed into sporting events but these bring the organisers into conflict. For some, the lifestyle is the core focus of their activity. For others, competition is the focus. Once again, people's identities help define and shape the direction of these activities, while global processes and corporations disseminate these activities.

KEY POINTS SUMMARY

- Since the Second World War, there have been a number of youth subcultures as young people have more disposable income, and seek to differentiate themselves from older generations.
- Subcultures are more fluid today as individuals can pick their influences from a wider range of media, cultures, influences and eras.
- Individual identity is articulated through our consumption choices: the types of music we listen to, the clothing we wear, the activities we do, the sports in which we participate.
- Many youth subcultures, particularly those associated with working-class young men, become 'folk devils' in the media. This creates a 'moral panic', which demonises these groups and calls for criminalisation of their activities.
- Some of these activities and objects become commercialised and sold back to a wider audience.
- Certain everyday activities, particularly sport, symbolise larger social groups, including cities, regions or countries.

KEY READING GUIDE

- Stan Cohen's influential analysis of the 1960s mods and rockers in *Folk Devils and Moral Panics* (1972) laid out how the media's role in amplifying deviance, particularly around the young. Often deviant examples are amplified or exaggerated to feed the media narrative which predicts that there will be future deviance, so calls on the government to focus their policing and legislation on tackling the 'problem'. This also attracts more people who enjoy transgression, or just simply wish to witness events, invariably bringing them into contact with the police, thus 'proving' the moral panic.
- Some groups wish to be seen as 'outsiders'. In *Outsiders* (1997) Howard Becker suggested that jazz musicians wished to be seen as transgressive and deviant, so that they did not conform to

the mediocre, boring everyday lives of the people they played for. Becker identified the importance of 'labelling' behaviour as deviant. It was not the person who was deviant, but the result of their activity.

- The collection of studies in *Resistance Through Rituals* (Hall and Jefferson, 1976) addressed a wide variety of subcultures from skinheads and rastas to girls' bedroom culture (as often girls' activities were not done in public). All took a similar approach – that subcultures were acts of working-class resistance against wider authority and consumer practices. Engaging in these activities was a way of asserting oneself within a collective.

- *Beyond A Boundary* (1963) regularly tops the lists of greatest sport books of all time. C.L.R. James manages to write a history of cricket that is not about cricket. He highlights the importance of sport throughout history, and it's importance to himself, his family, his community and the whole islands of the West Indies.

- In *Pitch Invasion: Adidas, Puma and the Making of Modern Sport* (2006), journalist Barbara Smit wrote a highly readable account of the rivalry between Adolph and Rudolph Dassler and how they influenced sport, governing bodies and wider culture.

Note

[1] www.dailymail.co.uk/sport/article-2112899/London-2012-Olympics-Plastic-Brits-insult-Games--Des-Kelly.html

3

Race, ethnicity and migration

Immigration has been at the centre of political wrangling in the UK and more widely for decades, but even more so since the referendum on the UK's membership of the EU, the European refugee 'crisis', and increasingly heated national and global debates about the benefits of multicultural societies. Populist movements across Europe and the US have brought to the fore questions about the impact immigration is having on national identity and wellbeing. Campaigns from those on the right of the political spectrum have suggested that immigration detrimentally impacts national security, the healthcare system, the economy and social cohesion. In contrast, studies show positive economic and cultural benefits of migration.[1] This chapter unpicks the current focus on migration and how understanding race and ethnicity is important in a multicultural society.

The Vote Leave campaign in the 2016 EU referendum suggested that 'Immigration will continue out of control putting public services like the NHS under strain.'[2] Alongside this, Nigel Farage, then leader of the UK Independence Party (UKIP), unveiled a 'Grassroots Out' campaign poster that showed a long queue of Syrian refugees (that were heading to Germany) with the phrase 'Breaking Point: the EU has failed us all'.[3] Messages such as this were instrumental in swaying the vote. The EU referendum also revealed the stark polarisation within the UK between its cities and surrounding regions. Areas with foreign-born citizens were congregated around the cities. Yet support for UKIP, a party that was known for its anti-immigration stance, was found in those areas where there were few immigrants.[4]

This raised the question as to whether fear of immigration and dislike of immigrants is borne of personal experiences so much as negative media discourse.

Box 3.1: What are 'British values'?

According to Ofsted (the Office for Standards in Education, Children's Services and Skills), the fundamental British values are: democracy; the rule of law; individual liberty; mutual respect for and tolerance of those with different faiths and beliefs, and for those without. These values are encouraged and promoted within all British schools. They have, however, been at the centre of debate about belonging and identity in the UK. The increase in focus on British values has been attributed to the growing ethnic diversity in British society, and used as justification for stringent immigration policy. This argument, however, overlooks how Britain and 'Britishness' were formed through a relationship with other nations and cultures, from empire through to contemporary processes of globalisation. Muslim communities have been particularly targeted, framed in the media as threats to British values – extremist, fundamentalist and radical, the polar opposite of tolerant and respectful of democracy. This has not only increased general antipathy towards Muslims in the UK, but has also fuelled hate crimes and far right support against them.

Headlines post-EU referendum persist about immigrants taking 'British' jobs and undermining 'British culture'. The British citizenship 'Life in the United Kingdom' test was introduced in 2002, a requirement for anyone seeking permanent residency in the UK. Questions test knowledge of key historical buildings in the UK, the religious history of the UK, the structure of the UK Parliament, and information about key historical British figures. A new 'British values test' was introduced in 2018, however, with a requirement for candidates to have a higher level of English proficiency and an understanding not so much of British history and customs, but the sorts of 'liberal values' (outlined in Box 3.1) that define British society.

With the emergent Brexit Party, founded in early 2019, populism based on a 'return' to British sovereignty cloaked in the language of democracy continues to dominate the current UK political scene. Like UKIP, the Brexit Party is founded on antipathy to the EU and the 'establishment', in other words the political elite who have failed to deliver a clean and timely break with Europe for the UK. Despite leader Nigel Farage stating that the Brexit Party delivers a clean break from the far right ideologies of UKIP (his former party whose campaigning fuelled the fire of the 'Leave' vote in the 2016 EU referendum), it still takes aim at the same perceived enemies, with immigrants and immigration again being at the front of the firing line of discontent.

Another reason for heightened scrutiny around immigration in Europe was the start of the so-called 'Refugee Crisis'. A record 1.2 million refugees sought asylum in the EU in 2015 – more than double the previous year – and represented the largest mass movement of people since the Second World War.[5] Most of these people were fleeing war and terrorism in Syria, Iraq and Afghanistan. Across significant parts of Europe, people were clearly saying 'Refugees Welcome'. The emotion of the situation was captured in a photograph of Alan Kurdi, a 3-year-old Syrian child, who drowned with his mother and brother while attempting to flee from Turkey to Greece in order to seek asylum with family in Vancouver in September 2015. The photo of Alan Kurdi face down in the water went around the world. In contrast to US sociologist and war crimes expert Stjepan Meštrović – who argued that we lived in a 'post emotional society' where people no longer emotionally connect with global suffering (1997) – the image of a dead child provoked widespread outpouring of support to refugees. Five days later the then British Prime Minister David Cameron promised to take 20,000 refugees over five years. To put this into context, Germany was taking that quantity in a weekend. As the UK had opted out of EU discussions on resettlement of refugees, they were not obliged to take more. Not all of the British population were and are so supportive of refugees and asylum seekers, however. Newspapers like the *Daily Mail* and *Daily Express* regularly ran front pages declaring the UK's borders to be under threat from refugees, particularly from those who were living in the makeshift camp called 'the Jungle' in Calais (cleared in October 2016). These fears still abound with continuing rumours that more migrant camps – often framed in the tabloids as headquarters for gangs seeking to smuggle individuals across borders – will emerge in Europe.[6]

Against this backdrop, hate crimes have proliferated. European nationals and those with perceived racial or ethnic difference from the majority population - particularly those of Muslim heritage – are being targeted with very public abuse. Videos show people shouting racist abuse or comments like 'go home'. *The Independent* found that hate crimes involving racial and religious discrimination increased by 23 per cent in the 11 months after the EU referendum (roughly July 2016 to June 2017).[7] *The Guardian* reported that areas of Kent such as Ramsgate, an area that voted overwhelmingly to leave the EU, experienced a particularly sharp increase in not only hate crime but also in everyday racism.[8]

The 'Go Home' vans commissioned by then Home Secretary (and later Prime Minister) Theresa May in 2015 were indicative of the 'Hostile Environment' that not only immigrants – legal and 'illegal' – but all racial and minority ethnic experiences in the UK. There are similarities here with the sorts of bordering tactics proposed by US President Donald Trump, including the wall between the US and Mexico (not to mention his Twitter comments in July 2019 telling four US Democratic congresswomen of colour to 'go back' to their countries from which they supposedly came). Israeli sociologist Nira Yuval-Davis (2011) talks about 'everyday bordering'. This is the way in which borders are constructed not only at the point where countries meet, but also in discourses, attitudes, institutions, the media and ideology. Government agencies like the UK Home Office monitor movements of peoples across borders along with hospitals, universities, schools and private companies and also determine who does and doesn't belong in a country.

As Jamaican-British cultural theorist Stuart Hall mentioned, for some, identity is about difference and when confronted with different culture, religion, language or skin colour, some feel that their identity is threatened. These feelings often find expression in racism. Discussions about culture often subsume discussions about race, however – when we are talking about immigration, asylum, ethnic diversity, multiculturalism and integration, more often than not race is the subtext. Migration, refugees and racism are wrapped up varying and conflicting processes of globalisation, history and identity. This chapter will account for the development and changes in migration since the Second World War, and how race relations and discourse have developed since. Again, we can see a pattern. Early migrants to the UK came from the former colonies as the country tried to rebuild. Since the 1980s there has been what sociologist and migration expert Stephen Castles (2009) calls 'a globalisation of migration' with more countries affected. This has coincided in the UK with de-industrialisation and a changing economy. As mentioned earlier, many of these new forms of migration are centred around the cities. Yet immigration has become highly politicised in every area of the UK, and across Western Europe and North America. And among all of this, questions of race, ethnicity, identity and belonging persist.

Migration in Britain

Migration is not new; human beings have always moved to find new opportunities. The history of British immigration, for example, stretches across centuries with Roman occupation, the settlement of the Saxons, Vikings and Normans, global trade-driven migration in the 12th to 15th centuries, and slavery and political migration from Western and Eastern Europe in the 19th century. After the Second World War, immigration from Commonwealth citizens ushered in a new age of migration in the 20th century. It also shouldn't be forgotten that migration is not one-way. Since the 19th century, thousands of British people have moved to North America,

Argentina, Australia and New Zealand, to Africa and India, and through the European Union.

Migration can have a dramatic impact on society. The 'refugee crisis' and the UK's decision to leave the EU are two of the most noteworthy events in recent European history and both are linked to migration. The high point of international migration was during the period from 1850 to the First World War, what Hatton and Williamson (1998) call the 'age of mass migration'. This coincided with dramatic social upheaval in Europe as many economies made their transition from rural agricultural societies to urban industrial ones. Many, like the Irish, moved because of food shortages and hardships felt through British rule. This period was really a period of transatlantic migration as people moved from Europe to North and South America. It should also not be forgotten that the other mass movement of people was also transatlantic, but this was forced migration in the slave trade from West Africa to the Caribbean and North America, followed by indentured workers from India. Since the Second World War migration has involved many more of the world's regions; it has expanded since the 1980s through easier access to communications and transport. People migrate with their families or to join their friends and families, as it is easier to find work and establish a new life when you have trusted people to guide you. There are also established migratory routes, particularly around certain forms of labour.

Despite this, the vast majority of human beings remain in their countries of birth. Migration is the exception, not the rule. People tend to move not individually, but in groups. Their departure may have considerable consequences for their area of origin. Remittances (money sent home) by migrants may improve living standards and encourage economic development. In the country of immigration, settlement is closely linked to employment opportunities and is almost always concentrated in industrial and urban areas, where the impact on the receiving communities is considerable. Migration thus affects not only the migrants themselves but also the sending and receiving societies (Castles, 2009).

As these movements are influenced by global factors, the causes and effects can be varied and conflicting. The EU referendum debate centred on the free movement of EU citizens who could work freely in the UK under EU law. Yet much of the fallout highlighted how some leave voters were actually voting as such to keep non-EU citizens out of the UK. One voter said that he voted leave to 'stop Muslims coming into the UK'.[9] While there are European Muslims, the implication was not placed on the European origins of these migrants. Again, global events help to explain why Muslims have become the immigrant 'folk devil'. Significant terrorist events, notably the 9/11 attacks on New York in 2001, propelled the global consciousness onto Islamic terrorism. The subsequent 'war on terror' by the US, the UK and their NATO allies has reinforced this division. Wars in Afghanistan and Iraq in 2003 were launched in an attempt to defeat Al Qaeda. The perpetrator of the 9/11 attacks, Osama Bin Laden, was eventually traced to Pakistan and killed by the US Special Forces in 2011. The Chilcot Inquiry into the UK's involvement in the Iraq invasion highlighted that war was not inevitable and destabilised the region. Other Islamic groups also emerged in Iraq and Syria, notably the Islamic State. Individuals inspired by Al Qaeda and the Islamic State have killed hundreds across the UK, Belgium, France, Germany, Turkey, Pakistan, Nigeria and Iraq, among others, in recent years. The result is that Muslims are seen as different from 'our' way of life, even though these individuals are in the minority among Muslims, and other nations (including the US and UK) have engaged in conflict without that being seen as a result of their religion or ethnicity.

Migration is not just from one social, ethnic or religious group. Some nations owe their existence to migration. The 'classical countries of immigration' include Argentina, Brazil, Australia, New Zealand, Canada and the US, as they comprise a majority of non-indigenous peoples. Some European nations have traditionally been seen as countries of emigration, such as Ireland, Italy, Greece and Spain. Elsewhere there are longstanding migratory patterns; for example, many African workers move to Southern Africa to work in the mines. The Middle East attracts workers from India, Pakistan and Bangladesh to work on the oil fields (or on football stadiums in the case of Qatar). Political turmoil and conflict have also led many countries in this region to be sources of refugees, notably Afghanistan, Iraq and Syria.

Box 3.2: The concept of 'diaspora space'

The functional definition of a diaspora is a scattered global population which has its ethnic origin in a separate, specific geographical location. Race scholar Avtar Brah (1996) talks about 'diaspora space' – the point where the categories of 'us' and 'them' are contested, where questions of belonging and otherness come to the fore. Diasporas constitute institutions in their own right, comprising their own networks, businesses, cultures and communities. However, diasporic people often experience a deep sense of rootlessness and isolation, even if they have been inhabiting an 'alien' space for many generations. They carry their migration experiences with them, subject to emotions that stretch from longing and nostalgia to pain and trauma, depending on why and how they relocated, and the way they are treated in their new homelands. Their experiences are also often implicated within wider historical and ongoing contemporary processes of colonisation, globalisation and migration.

The UK is a good example of migration in post-war Europe. As each nation sought to rebuild, migrant labour was favoured. France, the Netherlands and the UK looked to their former colonies, while Germany drew on workers from Turkey. Adverts were sent around the Commonwealth to invite workers to come to the UK. Thanks to its colonial past, the UK had a long history of migration from outside of Europe. Despite this long history, the arrival of the ship the *Empire Windrush* in 1948 became symbolic of a new form of migration as it transported West Indian migrants answering the call for jobs. Others came from the Indian subcontinent, particularly after the crisis of the partition of India in 1947 and South Asians from Uganda arrived after Idi Amin expelled them in 1972. Other groups came from Hong Kong, Australia and New Zealand. Migration from Africa was relatively low during this period. Despite the development of vast diasporas (defined in Box 3.2) over decades, the 2018 crisis in the UK government surrounding Windrush was indicative of the ways in which even the citizenship status of longstanding British citizens with roots in former British Commonwealth countries can come under question in the 'Hostile Environment'.

These migrants were coming for work so they went to the locations where there were jobs. This was a period of state support for industry and public investment in the economy. Migrants from Pakistan brought their textile skills to work in the mill towns of Lancashire and Yorkshire. Other South Asian and Caribbean migrants went to work in the NHS as nurses or doctors, or on public transport.

Figure 3.1: Monday 30 April 2018. Protestors from Global Justice Now demonstrate outside the Home Office in London demanding an end to the Hostile Environment policy, ahead of parliamentary debate on the Windrush scandal.

Source: © David Mirzoeff/Global Justice Now, www.flickr.com/photos/wdm/42061319872

As the comedian Paul Sinha said in relation to why his parents moved to the UK rather than the US: 'in the 1960s in Birmingham, Alabama, you weren't allowed onto the bus if you were a person of colour; in Birmingham, England, you were allowed to drive the bus!'[10] Perceived challenges to national identity were raised as early as the 1960s. Whereas citizens from Commonwealth countries had previously been granted extensive rights to migrate to the UK, the Conservative government introduced the Commonwealth Immigrants Act of 1962 that limited the number of migrants coming from the former colonies through the use of government-issued employment vouchers. The 1968 Act that followed introduced the 'partial link' criteria – immigrants had to prove a prior familial connection with a UK citizen. The Immigration Act of 1971 introduced work permits as a condition for immigration into the UK. As recession hit in the 1970s, and the economy restructured in the 1980s, immigrant communities increasingly became targets of racism, which will be considered later. After the 1979 election the Conservative Party leader Margaret Thatcher played on public fear and insecurity by describing non-white immigration as the 'enemy within', capable of swamping British culture and values (Solomos, 2003). Even today, as mentioned earlier, this rhetoric is still used.

Since the 1980s there has been a dramatic change in international migration. In *The Age of Migration* (2009), Stephen Castles identifies six different ways in which migration has changed:

- There has been a 'globalisation of migration' with more countries affected and with groups from different ethnic backgrounds.
- There has been an 'acceleration of migration' as people around the world become more aware of migratory routes, which places a challenge on government policy.
- Nations also face a 'differentiation of migration' with a range of migrants arriving. Rather than one type of migrant, there are those who come to study, for temporary work, for settlement or as refugees seeking asylum. These numbers vary depending on context.

- There has been a marked 'feminisation of migration' as more women are migrating to join partners or as part of the labour market. Women are also more likely to be trafficked, particularly around sex work.
- With the growing 'refugee crisis' there is a 'proliferation of migration transition'. More countries are becoming transit locations as migrants pass through them.
- Finally, as we have seen with the EU referendum, there is a 'politicisation of migration' as national and international policies and agreements become central.

Box 3.3: A points-based migration system

The UK's point-based system for immigration selects immigrants on a tiered basis, based on their language proficiency, educational credentials, age and work experience. It was introduced in 2008 to regulate immigration from outside the European Economic Area, to restore public trust in immigration control, and to eliminate racial bias by facilitating a more meritocratic system of immigration. It has, however, led to skilled shortages in some industries such as construction and the NHS. It is biased against those in what are deemed as low-skilled roles such as service and caregiving roles, predominantly taken up by women.

As educated migrants move to the global cities, new migratory networks have opened. These are a group of what Australian cultural studies professor Nikos Papastergiadis (2000) calls 'skilled transients' – bankers, consultants, academics, engineers, and technicians – who use their skills wherever the global economy requires them. Class is a significant factor here. Global cities compete to attract the highly skilled and seek to privilege those with money and skills. The points-based immigration system (briefly outlined in Box 3.3) privileges those with the skills that are required in the new global cities.

This does nothing to alleviate the polarised economy in the UK that excludes many from the labour market. Low-skilled migrant workers often work in jobs that are seen as undesirable by British workers. The mobility of migrants who cannot work, or struggle to find work, is bounded by welfare state restrictions which afford citizenship privileges on the basis of their labour contributions (Anderson, 2013). Despite this, global cities remain focal points as migrants still flock to seek work in the service sector in shops, restaurants, hotels and hairdressers. In many cases these become places where immigrants invest and establish their own businesses, and ultimately place roots.

Box 3.4: Immigration and the UK's National Health Service

Writing in the *British Medical Journal* in 2016, social geographer Danny Dorling outlined how immigration discourse has long scapegoated non-British migrants and even non-native British citizens as the basis for the decline in the NHS. He stated:

> the underlying reason for worsening health and declining living standards was not immigration but ever growing economic inequality and the public spending cuts that accompanied austerity. Almost all other European countries tax more effectively, spend more on health, and do not tolerate our degree of economic inequality. To distract us from these national failings, we have been encouraged to blame immigration and the EU.

Somewhat ironically, migrant labour is central to the functioning of the NHS. Only since June 2018 have stringent visa restrictions been lifted for EU medical professionals given the need to tackle healthcare worker shortages.

Immigrant workers to the UK are more likely to be younger and making a positive net contribution to the economy through taxation and reduced costs on the health (see Box 3.4) and welfare systems[11] (Hochlaf and Franklin, 2016). When certain politicians state that they want an open and honest debate on immigration, they are generally talking about it in negative terms. Sociologists can help to link immigration to bigger global factors and understand why immigration has become the scapegoat for these factors.

Immigration and ethnicity are often the most obvious markers of difference within a community. This can become more pronounced when an area is going through a process of de-industrialisation. Those with desirable skills can, in this global economy, move to where the jobs exist, often in global cities. They take their incomes and investments with them and this can have a dramatic effect on local economies. This leaves a polarisation along ethnic lines. Consequently, immigrants and people from minority ethnic groups are targeted as the reason for the decline, or the reason that the local population are no longer in work.

Immigration has a positive effect on local communities and economies. Wadsworth et al (2016: 2) demonstrate that

> areas of the UK with large increases in EU immigration did *not* suffer greater falls in the jobs and pay of UK-born workers. The big falls in wages after 2008 are due to the global financial crisis and a weak economic recovery, not to immigration,

with changes in wages and joblessness for less educated UK-born workers showing 'little correlation with changes in EU immigration'. Effectively, the economic problems faced by de-industrialised communities are not due to immigration, but by an employment market that does not support the skills of large sections of British society in the locations they live.

In trying to develop a sociological imagination, it is important to move away from the obvious, 'common sense' foci of people's anger or confusion, and to critically question the rhetoric of politicians and parts of the media. It's also important to understand the feelings of the people who are affected. Immigration is an emotive topic. Emotions are an important part of human interaction.

The 'refugee crisis'

Refugees are accepted in the UK if they have fled their own country as a result of persecution based on race, religion, nationality or political stance, according to the Geneva Convention on refugees. An asylum seeker, by contrast, is someone who has applied to the Home Office for refugee status or a similar form of protection, and is waiting for a decision on their application. The UK takes far fewer asylum applications than other EU countries: less than Germany, France, Italy, Greece and Spain. In fact, according to the United Nations Refugee Agency UNHCR (2019),[12] 80 per cent of all refugees are hosted in developing regions. This may be surprising, however, given the public discourse on refugees and asylum seekers.

Refugees and asylum seekers have generally been framed as 'problem' in the popular media and wider public (McDonald and Billings, 2007) over recent decades, another example of a 'folk devil' that has led to a 'moral panic' (Cohen, 1972). They are often depicted as entering the UK in swarms, simultaneously taking people's jobs *and* claiming welfare that they are not entitled to. This has been exacerbated by the Immigration and Asylum Act 1999, which dispersed refugees throughout the country, often to areas that had the cheapest housing (so the poorest areas). According to 2017 Home Office data, more than half of all asylum seekers housed by the government are done so in the poorest third of the country. The richest third of the country houses just a tenth of all asylum seekers.[13]

The placing of refugees predominantly within areas struggling from a lack of economic investment has often led to conflict within communities (D'Onofrio and Munk, 2004), with the assumption being that refugees are given disproportionate amounts of state benefits. In actuality, the weekly level of financial support for asylum seekers is half of unemployment benefit (in the UK this is currently £36.96 per person seeking asylum[14]). Asylum seekers are not allowed to claim benefits or work and, on being given refugee status, have just a month to establish themselves before being evicted from asylum accommodation.[15] As we shall see in the next chapter, welfare dependents have become an increasing 'folk devil' and the neoliberal state has reduced welfare in order to 'encourage' claimants to find work. This is problematic for asylum seekers, as the law does not allow them to work. They have half of an amount of money that is designed to make people poorer to incentivise them to work. Despite this, asylum seekers and refugees continue to be portrayed negatively in public and political discourse.

C. Wright Mills highlighted how developing a sociological imagination entailed linking broader aspects of society, history and biography. It is no coincidence that most recent refugee movements to Europe are from Syria, Iraq and Afghanistan. These three countries have been devastated by conflict for decades, and particularly since the US and UK invasions of Iraq and Afghanistan in 2003. Other countries from which thousands are fleeing include Eritrea, Sudan and South Sudan, which have also endured decades of conflict. Many of these refugees enter Europe by undertaking the dangerous crossing across the Sahara and enter Italy through Libya, another country that has been the victim of regime change as a result of US and Western European military action. The focus on refugees entering Europe ignores just how many refugees are living in neighbouring countries (such as Turkey, Uganda, Pakistan and Lebanon), or who are internally displaced peoples. The UNHCR identified that there are an unprecedented 65 million people who have been displaced and, of these, over 27 million are internally displaced.[16] This puts the 20,000 Syrians David Cameron promised to house in the UK into perspective. Many refugees wish to return home after the causes for their displacement cease, which is why they stay close to home. But conflicts are becoming more protracted and complex which creates difficulties. Aligned with this, as we saw in the previous section, migration has become politicised, so opportunities for asylum are diminishing.

Refugees became a significant global feature in the 1970s. Although there have been mass movements of people fleeing their homeland, such as Russians leaving after the Revolution, Armenians fleeing Turkey after the Armenian genocide, or Jews escaping Nazism, there was no clear international framework governing them. With the formation of the United Nations in 1945, and more importantly, the UNHCR in 1950, there were opportunities to create an international legal framework, and the agreement of the 1951 Convention relating to the Status of Refugees was signed in Geneva. The focus of the UN definition of a refugee, however, is always on leaving one's nation, so does not cover internally displaced peoples. And it leaves stateless people, such as Palestinians, in a difficult situation. The forced displacement of millions of Palestinians during the conflicts with Israel in 1967 and the 1970s saw the beginnings of contemporary 'refugee crises'.

Sustained conflicts, particularly in South East Asia and Africa as a result of rapid decolonisation, saw refugee numbers increase. Austerity measures inflicted by the Washington Consensus of the International Monetary Fund and World Bank also contributed to displacement of people in Africa (Zolberg et al, 1989). Rarely did these 'refugee crises' affect Europe as those affected did not have the means to reach Europe (except for groups like South Asians fleeing Uganda in 1972, for example). Occasionally, political refugees from Communist countries sought refuge in the West, but not in great numbers (although many from Cuba made it to the US). The Balkans war in the early 1990s dramatically changed things in Europe as millions fled the former Yugoslavia. While refugee numbers fell at the start of the 21st century, this was mainly due to nation states limiting the numbers of those seeking asylum (Castles, 2009).

The role of the state is important. While national governments across Western Europe and North America have attempted to 'roll back' the state from intervention in welfare and the economy, they have reinforced borders and security. This gives rise to the paradox of a globalisation of migration alongside a tightening of borders. There has also been an increase in those trying to circumvent these restrictions – what has become termed 'illegal immigration'. This has led to the development of an entire industry that tries to help people migrate and circumvent borders. These people traffickers overloaded the boat carrying Alan Kurdi that capsized. This then leads to a further tightening of borders.

Efforts by nation states to regulate and control migration are at an all-time high. There is a huge amount of public pressure, driven partially by media coverage, for political leadership to take a hard line on traffickers and 'illegal immigration'. Regulation on an international scale has centred on extensive treaties, bilateral agreements and international diplomacy. This is where the EU was important for the UK because it was part of these agreements. The British government was allowed to move the UK border to Calais in order to prevent 'illegal immigrants' from gaining access to the UK. This border is policed by the French police and allowed the UK to keep a certain amount of distance from the frontline issues with migrant encampment in Calais in 2015 and 2016. However, this has not diminished the extent to which refugees and migrants have been problematised and politicised over recent years. As conflict and economic strife rages across the Middle East and Africa in particular, it is likely that the 'refugee crisis' will continue be a defining feature of European politics for a number of years.

Multiculturalism, ethnic diversity and racism

The movement of people can bring a sharp contrast to how local and national populations see themselves. Identity is about similarities and differences with others. When we are confronted with difference, it can accentuate our sense of self. But it can also lead us to question what we have in common. People migrating can have different backgrounds, different political, cultural or religious traditions, and possibly speak a different language. Often the most visible markers of difference are skin colour, hair and dress. We present our identities through the performance of our clothing. This helps differentiate us and present what we see as important. It is for this reason that the hijab and burqa have become such potent symbols. They clearly mark difference and affiliation to a culture and religion, which in the post 9/11 environment has become politically charged. Yet this also calls into question existing national traditions.

The UK has held a multicultural approach to diverse ethnic groups. This has developed from the British tradition of liberalism that called for minimum governmental involvement in individuals' lives. This broadly accepts different cultural groups. This contrasts with the French assimilationist approach. While France grants full citizenship rights, it expects full loyalty to the state – all citizens (must) become French. It is for this reason that the hijab has been banned in France, as it goes against the 'national myth' of cultural unity in belief and practices (Castles, 2000). Despite this clear cultural contrast between France and the UK, some British politicians and members of the public still expect assimilation, rather than integration. The latter requires a two-way process where the dominant culture accepts certain aspects of the diverse cultures and adapts accordingly. In the UK, these sorts of laws have been seen as un-British and an unwelcome and unnecessary intrusion into people's personal lives. Yet, as Castles (2009: 15) states,

> Immigration often takes place at the same time as economic restructuring and far-reaching social change. People whose conditions of life are already changing in an unpredictable way often see the newcomers as the cause of insecurity.

There have been targeted policies that seek to integrate; yet this can lead to resentment from pre-existing communities who feel that someone else is getting the benefits. This is tied into economic as well as social discontent as many feel these newcomers receive a disproportionate share of increasingly limited economic resources. Once again, however, we return to the often forgotten point that successive national governments have failed to invest in de-industrialised communities and this leads to immigrants being scapegoated and targeted.

Perceived difference can lead to open and subtle forms of racism. The late 1960s and early 1970s saw a raft of social legislation to challenge discrimination. The Race Relations Acts of 1965 and 1968 were the first pieces of legislation in the UK to address racial discrimination. They outlawed discrimination on the 'grounds of colour, race, or ethnic or national origins' in public places and made it illegal to refuse housing, employment or public services to a person on the grounds of colour, race, ethnic or national origins. Before then there had been signs in landlords' windows declaring 'No blacks, No Irish, No dogs'. British television still had explicitly racist or stereotypical shows into the 1970s when there was a wider public backlash. Explicit racism continued in football stadiums into the 1990s, with traces still there. And racism still exists in subtle forms in most institutions and areas of public life.

Box 3.5: Enoch Powell and the white working class

Enoch Powell led the critiques of the 1965 and 1968 Race Relations Acts, asserting the rights of white English people to engage in discrimination. He strategically positioned himself as the champion of the white working classes, positing them as victims of untethered immigration with their towns and services changed beyond recognition, and without their consent (Solomos, 2003). He represented black people as the embodiment of noise, uncleanliness and violence, and most worryingly as the cause of the decline of the prospects of the white working classes. Despite this call to arms, only sporadic protests occurred in support of Powell and his comments, and he eventually withdrew from political life. However, his tactics of scapegoating immigrants and dividing the working classes along racial lines are still employed by those on the right and the far right.

At the same time as the passing of race relations legislation there was a politicisation of race. The Conservative politician Enoch Powell's infamous 'rivers of blood' speech in 1968 links to many themes that re-emerged throughout the EU referendum (see Box 3.5). The undercurrent of 'taking our country' back linked to comments made by Enoch Powell about the country losing its sense of identity. Taking his title from a National Front leaflet, British social theorist Paul Gilroy's *There Ain't No Black in the Union Jack* (1987) suggests that the history of Britain and its empire is imagined as one homogeneous white and Christian culture. All other culture, including black culture, is set in opposition to this, not just by those advocating a white monoculture, but those engaged in anti-racism. As Gilroy (1987: 13) argues, 'culture does not develop along ethnically absolute lines ... new definitions of what it means to be black emerge from raw materials provided by black populations elsewhere in the diaspora'. In *The Black Atlantic* (1993), Gilroy suggests that there is no essential or authentic 'black' culture because it is rooted in transnational, global networks that can be traced throughout history, from African history, through slavery to contemporary forms of black culture. In a globalised world, we are saturated with a variety of cultural forms. And for many people, they find solace in essentialised cultural forms.

Negative characterisations about a racial group when internalised and ingrained in the fabric of a society allow one racial and/or ethnic group to essentialise and thus dominate, or attempt to dominate, another set of people. This was the basis of many centuries of colonialism. European imperialists justified their colonisation through 'natural' superiority. New scientific discoveries and classifications at the time, like the theory of evolution, influenced this approach. This was more overt in the US where Jim Crow Laws specifically segregated people based on the colour of their skin and prevented them from voting until 1965. It was taken a step further in Nazi Germany where Germans were seen as a distinct race, while Roma and Jews were to be kept separate and then executed in the Holocaust.

Scientific racism declined in popularity and legitimacy from the second half of the 20th century. It is, however, making a reappearance as British science journalist Angela Saini argues in *Superior: The Return of Race Science* (2019). Divorcing race from biology does not mean race is no longer problematic. Most people would purport to be 'colourblind' nowadays, but does this mean racism no longer exists? With the growing awareness that race was a socially constructed category, there was also a growing awareness that skin colour should not be a determining factor. Culture once again becomes the defining marker of difference. If an identified group becomes repeatedly identified as not succeeding or conforming to a set of wider ideals, then it is attributed to cultural failings, rather than biological. The result is what Puerto Rican sociologist Eduardo Bonilla-Silva (2006) calls 'colourblind racism' in *Racism without Racists: Colorblind Racism and the Persistence of Racial Inequality in the United States*. There's an acknowledgement that one cannot attribute physical or intellectual ability or moral failings to skin colour. Yet this does not mean that someone is not racist because they don't 'see' the colour of somebody's skin. It just means that you're not very observant, as the comedian Reginald D. Hunter (2012) sardonically notes.

As discussed earlier, anti-discrimination legislation was introduced from 1965 and during the 1970s and 1980s to override some of the structural issues affecting minority ethnic groups. These policies became known as 'positive discrimination' and sought to provide access to opportunities, mainly in the public sector, for people of colour. In doing so it was acknowledged that institutions like the labour market, the housing sector and the welfare sector were structurally biased against racial minorities, and thus sought to rectify it. This coincided with a cultural movement called 'political correctness' that challenged many of the assumptions of race, gender and sexuality. This led to a backlash from those arguing that many of the claims made by minority groups are 'PC gone mad'. The implication is that no British state should tell people how to think. The irony is that 'PC' could also stand for 'politeness and civility', which are the most British of values. We should question why people who claim 'it's PC gone mad' seek to be abusive to others.

The colourblind approach to race and racism in the UK was challenged after the tragic murder of Stephen Lawrence in 1993. Lawrence was stabbed to death in a racially motivated attack in East London by some white men. After a long campaign by Lawrence's mother, Doreen, in 1998 the Labour government instigated a public inquiry into the investigation and trial, which gained unprecedented media and public attention. The 'Macpherson Report' published in 1999 identified significant failings in the Metropolitan Police, particularly around how they dealt with crimes involving race. Macpherson described the police force as 'institutionally racist' which 'can be seen or detected in processes, attitudes, and behaviour, which amount to discrimination through unwitting prejudice, ignorance, thoughtlessness, and racist stereotyping, which disadvantages minority ethnic people'. Not only were discriminatory attitudes towards minority ethnic groups prevalent and left unchecked, but also there was no crime in the UK that had 'race' as a motivation. This was rectified by the Crime and Disorder Act 1998 as part of the wider analysis of Stephen Lawrence's murder.

As with other areas of contemporary life, the government has liberalised society. Now that 'we' are colourblind, then there is a growing 'racial neoliberalism' as South African critical race theorist David Theo Goldberg writes in *The Threat of Race* (2009). Race is pushed away from public discussions and there is a suggestion we live in a 'post-racial' society where there are no structural obstacles for anyone to access jobs, education or health. Language has shifted where the term 'reverse racism' is directed at those who invoke race as a reason for pervading inequalities. As Goldberg (2009: 360, original emphasis) argues, 'Here racism is reduced in its supposed singularity to *invoking* race, not to its debilitating structural effects or the legacy of its ongoing unfair impacts.' As with other areas of neoliberalism, issues are individualised, they are never structural. If someone says something racist, then it is their individual act, not part of some wider social issue. The silence of significant sections of the media and politicians after the dramatic increase on hate crimes after the EU referendum reinforces this; those hate crimes were directed not only at those on the street but also at fellow politicians and journalists. These instances of abuse, graffiti and violence were attributed to individual perpetrators, not to the wider cultural or social environment that legitimated and empowered these individuals to behave in this manner.

The question of race and the concept of a post-racial (see Box 3.6) society emerged in the US around the Black Lives Matter movement formed in 2013. The movement grew out of a public awareness that a significant number of young black men were being shot dead by police, often over minor violations or in the course of routine questioning. The movement came to public prominence after riots in the Missouri town of Ferguson after a young black man, Michael Brown, was shot dead by a police officer in August 2014. The riot and continued unrest brought attention to the higher proportion of police stops on young black men. Black Lives Matter sought to challenge the institutional racism within the US police and used social media to raise awareness through the #blacklivesmatter hashtag. There was, however, a predictable backlash. The #alllivesmatter hashtag was used to suggest that there should not be a focus on black lives.

Box 3.6: What is 'post-racialism'?

Post-racialism is, in effect, a denial of the persistence of racism in contemporary society. It has been posed as an ideology – a system of thought and belief which seeks to transcend racial division, and distance society from the intolerance of the past, by trying to go beyond racism (Bobo 2011). In doing so, however, it fails to address the very real inbuilt continuing racism in institutions and everyday life. According to Burkhalter (2006) it preserves and normalises racial inequality by not exposing very real racist structures, actions and attitudes.

Reinforcing the belief in a post-racial world, some even suggested that it was racist to draw attention to the skin colour of the victims. #alllivesmatter misunderstands (at least) two very important aspects of race and racism. First, that it is a zero-sum game – if some group, be it female, gay, black or Asian is getting something then it means that it is to the detriment of someone else. Empowerment of others is not automatically to the detriment of the dominant (white) culture – if the US police stop shooting young black men, then it does not automatically mean that they will start shooting young white men. Second, calling 'racism' on Black Lives Matter for drawing attention to race fails to recognise and understand the ways in which people of colour are the repeated targets, both historically and contemporarily, of negative stereotyping, aggression and exclusion. Everyday microaggressions compound feelings of marginalisation. Only through understanding the lived experience of the victims is it possible to have a sensible discussion around race and racism. Projecting one's own experiences and beliefs onto someone else, especially if that person has a different gender, sexuality or skin colour, will ensure that we are not taking care to develop our sociological imagination. This is why 'critical race theory' (exemplified by the work of US sociologist and activist W.E.B Du Bois, see Box 3.7) is a useful way to understand issues around race and racism as it locates race and racisms within the wider power structures of society, while centralising the lived experiences of those affected.

Box 3.7: Du Bois and the concept of 'double consciousness'

W.E.B. Du Bois is seen a key thinker in critical race theory. He sought to put African-American lives and communities at the heart of his theories. Du Bois talked about 'double consciousness' in his 1903 publication *The Souls of Black Folk*. The concept describes the sort of identity conflicts experienced by black people in the US. He believed they embodied a divided identity, acutely aware of how they are seen through the lens of racial prejudice by mainstream, white society, as both American but ultimately Negro. Double consciousness is still important to our society to understand how difficult it is for marginalised individuals to reconcile their social identities.

KEY POINTS SUMMARY

- Migration is not a new phenomenon. The mass movement of peoples into and out of countries has been happening for centuries.
- Migration is often met with disproportionate media hype and the scapegoating and criminalisation of migrants. These reactions are exacerbated by economic insecurity.

- Racism occurs when groups are 'othered' on the basis of race, nationality or religion. It manifests in both every day and structural discrimination which persists in the UK despite claims we are now a 'post-racial' society.
- The backlash against anti-racist movements is couched in claims of reverse racism and 'political correctness gone mad', predominantly from dominant racial groups in society.

KEY READING GUIDE

- A comprehensive and all important critical overview of the history of race and racism can be found in John Solomos' *Race and Racism in Britain* (2003) which touches on social theory, policy, social movements and social change, all within the historical context of race relations in the UK.
- Gilroy's *There Ain't No Black in the Union Jack* (1987) is a key read for any budding critical race theorist, defining and analysing the relationship between race, ethnicity, class and ideas of the nation to understand exactly how racism manifests and persists over time.
- Bonilla-Silva carries out a similar project to Gilroy in *Racism without Racists: Colorblind Racism and the Persistence of Racial Inequality in America* (2006). This book critiques the 'colourblind approach' to dealing with race with reference to the US, seeking to understand exactly how racism – while being decried on a daily basis – continues to shape the lives of people of colour.
- In *Us and Them? The Dangerous Politics of Immigration Control* (2013) Bridget Anderson maps out the politics of immigration, particularly how and why both citizens and migrants are or are not deemed worthy of the privileges of membership to the 'community of value' comprised of 'Good Citizens'.
- Stephen Castles in *Ethnicity and Globalization* (2000) gives a comprehensive overview of global migration since 1945 – analysing the role of the labour market and policy responses,

along with ideas of citizenship, nation and culture – to understand the economic and social drivers and effects of contemporary migration.

Notes

[1] www.nature.com/articles/d41586-018-05507-0

[2] www.voteleavetakecontrol.org/briefing_immigration.html

[3] www.theguardian.com/politics/2016/jun/16/nigel-farage-defends-ukip-breaking-point-poster-queue-of-migrants

[4] www.telegraph.co.uk/news/politics/ukip/11539388/Mapped-where-is-Ukips-support-strongest-Where-there-are-no-immigrants.html

[5] http://ec.europa.eu/eurostat/documents/2995521/7203832/3-04032016-AP-EN.pdf/790eba01-381c-4163-bcd2-a54959b99ed6

[6] www.dailymail.co.uk/news/article-5300253/Fears-new-Calais-Jungle-Brussels.html

[7] www.independent.co.uk/news/uk/home-news/racist-hate-crimes-surge-to-record-high-after-brexit-vote-new-figures-reveal-a7829551.html

[8] www.theguardian.com/society/2018/oct/21/absolute-hell-kent-residents-speak-out-over-hate-surge

[9] www.huffingtonpost.co.uk/entry/eu-referendum muslims_uk_576e558ce4b08d2c563937ff

[10] Paul Sinha's Citizenship Test (2013) BBC Radio 4, 5 August.

[11] www.migrationobservatory.ox.ac.uk/briefings/fiscal-impact-immigration-uk

[12] www.unhcr.org/uk/figures-at-a-glance.html

[13] www.theguardian.com/world/2017/apr/09/its-a-shambles-data-shows-most-asylum-seekers-put-in-poorest-parts-of-britain

[14] www.gov.uk/asylum-support/what-youll-get

[15] www.refugee-action.org.uk/about/facts-about-refugees/

[16] www.unhcr.org/figures-at-a-glance.html

4

Class

There is a clear polarisation in British society over access to jobs, job security and income inequality. The informational economy around knowledge and service sector skills has concentrated job opportunities and wealth in major cities, particularly London. The drastic wealth disparities in Western societies were also exposed during the global financial crisis of 2007–08. Occupy, the multi-platform, anti-inequality social movement, reiterated this point by declaring that 'We are the 99%.' The movement highlighted the concentrating of global wealth in only 1 per cent of the world's population. As the neoliberal state has been restructured to facilitate global capitalism, rather than social provision, income inequalities have been exacerbated. This chapter outlines how class is another way that society differentiates between large groups of people and how this has changed since the 1950s.

Changes to class composition and identification are the other outcomes of the restructured economy. In 1990 the then UK Conservative Prime Minister John Major expressed his desire for a classless society as this would symbolise social mobility. Seven years later the Labour Deputy Prime Minister John Prescott is attributed to have said that 'We're all middle class now.' The comment was a reference to the growth of the service sector as an indication of the post-industrial society that the UK had become. The implication was that we were all wealthier because our employment prospects were changing. This political outlook links to traditional ideas of class based on economic wealth. It also conforms to some sociological analysis that will be addressed later in the chapter, particularly as it links back to arguments about the individualisation of society. These analyses don't take into account the various ways that class reproduces itself. In order to access opportunities to climb the social and economic ladder, we need to know the right people and have the right skills, knowledge and conversation topics. This aspect will be considered at the end of this chapter, as we look at a new area of research on class distinctions that draws on the work of the influential French sociologist Pierre Bourdieu.

The classic British model of class was epitomised in the satirical 1960s show *That Was The Week That Was* with comedians John Cleese, Ronnie Barker and Ronnie Corbett, all of differing heights, looking down and up to the others. The upper class was the ruling aristocracy, people who have been born into land, titles and money. Then there was the middle class working in 'white collar' professions that required a white shirt and tie. Below them, the working class engaged in manual, semi-skilled and unskilled labour in 'blue collar' jobs (based on the colour of their blue overalls). As with other everyday assumptions, sociology digs deeper and wider. The sociological imagination needs to take in the history and traditions of the UK that account for its specific class system. It also needs to understand individual's biographies and personal identities, while linking this to the wider political and economic changes that have affected society since the Second World War. We see a similar process occurring in relation to class as we see in relation to other forms of identity. What were considered 'traditional' and stable forms of identity have been broken down. In their place new groups and forms of identification – based on race, ethnicity, gender, sexuality, profession – have formed. While class is no longer the primary form of identification for many people, and others suggest that we are in a 'post-class' world or a 'classless society', class still retains a central place in sociological thought as we look at the impact of wider social changes on individuals' social status.

Classical sociological definitions of class predominantly focus on the economic aspects. German sociologist Max Weber (1978: 302) suggested that one's class is expressed through 'shared typical probability of procuring goods, gaining a position in life, and finding inner satisfaction'. This idea of obtaining goods in order to fulfil one's own identity and promote one's social position is clearly linked to economic opportunities. As Weber (1978: 928) said, 'class situation is market situation.' German philosopher, economist and social theorist Karl Marx also based class on economic opportunities. Despite opening Chapter 1 of the *Communist Manifesto* (written with his friend Friedrich Engels in 1848) with the line 'The history of all hitherto existing society is the history of class struggles' and the book being full of references to class, Marx did not elaborate a clear definition. For him, the exploitative relationship between workers (the proletariat) and the bourgeoisie (the owners of production) was of paramount importance. He did, however, distinguish between a 'class *in* itself' – workers who have a common relation to the means of production – and a 'class *for* itself' – a group who were conscious of their class position and mobilised politically because of it. For Marx, class consciousness became the major challenge for those seeking to transform their social position (see Box 4.1 for more discussion on this). However, Marx and Weber's focus on the economic bases of class relations obscures two important factors which determine an individual or a group's class position: personal connections, and knowledge and skills. As argued in Chapter 2, we are not isolated individuals but emotional social beings who form groups with likeminded people. Some of these will be through work, others through leisure activities, others as a result of culture or religion, for example. We tend to join the groups that we feel we 'fit' in. Some groups, however, confer higher social status and economic opportunities than others. If we don't have the cultural 'passports' to let us into these particular groups then it will be difficult to access the market position and the sort of lifestyles that certain forms of employment bring. This will be discussed later on in the chapter.

Box 4.1: Class consciousness versus class identity

Marx saw class consciousness as a key component for social change. Class consciousness is when workers identify as a united group and envisage an alternative society. In other words, it is a commitment to transformation from below, by those from below. As classes have become more fragmented in recent decades, we might ask whether class consciousness can be said to (still) exist. Most research has found that people tend to see themselves as members of a middling group of ordinary, working citizens. It is difficult to ascertain whether people think of themselves as working, middle or upper class let alone identify politically as such, because traditional sociological interviewing techniques would potentially put class at the forefront of the interviewee's mind in an unnatural, contrived way. Furthermore, class is often experienced through one's other social identities: gender, sexuality, race, ethnicity and disability. There are those who thus believe that identities like class can only be studied in context, through interactions and in real life situations. Skeggs (1997) also talks about the symbolic weight of class. Individuals have difficulties facing the reality of class inequality, and thus clearly expressing a class identity. This only again problematises the study of whether class has any personal, social and political meaning to individuals.

Individualisation and the underclass

In the introduction (and elsewhere in this book) it was highlighted that there is an argument that contemporary social life is increasingly fragmented and individualistic. Traditional forms of solidarity have broken down and we no longer identify with our communities or work colleagues. While identities have become more fluid, that is not to say that new ways of connecting with other people are not occurring. But as these traditional boundaries break down, there are some that suggest that we live in a post-class society, where the idea of belonging to the 'working classes' or the 'middle classes' doesn't hold the same sort of weight as it may have for previous generations. Class identity, like race and gender, was considered by seminal Jamaican-British cultural theorist Stuart Hall (1991) to be one among multiple forms of group identification. This does not suggest that class is not materially and culturally important. Simply that it is dependent on, and relative to, other forms of identification like – as we saw in Chapter 3 – race and ethnicity.

German sociologist Ulrich Beck calls class a 'zombie category' in that even though it is dead, it is still alive. In a 'risk society' (Beck, 1992), where global capitalism is transformed and affects our consumption, lifestyles and individual identities, class becomes redundant. As the individual reflexively constructs their own identity, then they are free to choose their own destiny. Beck (1992) calls this the 'elevator effect' where we have generally risen up in social quality. Yet this suggests that everyone has access to the same elevator.

Structural economic inequalities continue. Following the EU referendum in 2016, analysis showed that working-class people outside the main UK cities were more likely to have voted to leave. While elsewhere this book has argued that this is in large part due to structural issues including the restructuring of the British economy in relation to globalisation, other analyses do not. Neoliberal and individualistic accounts suggest that the reason for individual and family poverty is due to cultural or individual failings, not structural factors. It can be argued that as the neoliberal state seeks to reduce the welfare state in order to permit the free movement of capital, then it is in the interests of those in power to place the blame on those who have been affected by the change in policies. This can be seen in the 1990s in the UK when a moral panic with regard to 'single mothers' grew. They signified the declining morality of the nuclear family (which will be touched on in Chapter 6) as well as the parasitic way that they relied on the welfare state. For a section of the right-wing media and politicians, single mothers symbolised everything that was wrong about modern Britain. Yet the analysis did not place the blame at the restructuring of the economy that had happened over the previous decade. It was blamed on individual failings and a culture of laziness among the poorer sections of society, or the so-called 'underclass' (see Box 4.2).

Box 4.2: The myth of the underclass

The underclass has been referred to by politicians throughout successive Labour and Conservative governments as 'feral', 'troubled', 'broken' and 'dysfunctional' and has been immortalised through the derogatory term 'chav'. Images of hooded youths circulated during the 2011 London Riots only further entrenched the image of the UK poor as young, immoral and violent, rather than impoverished and disenfranchised. The criminalisation of the poor has created an image of a lazy, work-shy section of society to whom most social ills can be attributed. The concept of an underclass can be dated back to the mid-1800s, a social group defined through generations by high levels of unemployment and social instability but framed as inherently problematic in terms of its antisocial behaviours and lack of 'mainstream values'. Research has since shown, however, that this conceptualisation of the underclass is a myth (Tyler, 2013). The stigmatisation of certain social groups allows the government – with the help of the media – to frame, in the public imagination, structural issues of economic inequality and poverty as a cultural and psychological problem.

In *The Emerging British Underclass* (1990), US political scientist Charles Murray identified a similar trend to what was happening in his country. Single mothers living on welfare in inner-city areas would produce a culture separate from the values of wider society. These children would grow up in an environment without the motivation or desire to work, have poor educational prospects and the result would be crime. This group would be called 'the underclass' and they were identified in three ways: illegitimacy, violent crime and voluntary drop out from the labour force. Murray drew his conclusions from observations from the US, which predominantly focused on a racialised image of the black single mother. Despite this, he did not draw the same racialised conclusion for the UK, choosing to focus on the gendered aspect. Murray observed that illegitimacy had rapidly increased since the 1970s and that the majority of this was concentrated in the lowest social class. Murray suggested that this relationship links to the lack of employment. He also used violent crime to support his thesis. As young men predominantly are the perpetrators, he argues that this was due to them not having 'father figures'. Finally, Murray's focus was on those who choose to take unemployment benefit, rather than working. Again, Murray was focusing on the role of paid work for men, rather than women,

Figure 4.1: A hooded 'youth' photographed against the backdrop of the 2011 UK Riots

Source: Open Democracy, www.flickr.com/photos/opendemocracy/7609229236

and doesn't acknowledge the unpaid work that single mothers or women in general do.

Despite the growing rhetoric of a classless society, Charles Murray was retaining a class-based analysis. Yet this wasn't about class consciousness or structural issues. It was about placing the blame on the underclass for their own predicament. Although Murray's statistical analysis drew conclusions from correlated statistics, correlation does not equal causation. Structural analyses are important, or you risk reducing social problems to individual behaviours. To develop a full sociological imagination, we have to look at what has happened to the jobs, housing and policing in these areas, as well as the broader political and economic climate. We should also listen to the lived experience of people living in these situations, as British sociologist Lisa McKenzie does in *Getting By* (2015). She presents what US sociologist Alvin Gouldner would call 'underdog sociology' and gives a voice to those without a voice. In this way we learn about wider social issues and inequalities.

Successive Labour (1997–2010, sometimes called 'New Labour') and Conservative (2010 onwards) governments have targeted those claiming welfare to incentivise them getting a job. The post-industrial economy privileges certain skills. As low-skilled work has been outsourced to a global labour market, this does not automatically permit access to all individuals in the UK to new economic opportunities. Likewise, as education is central to the post-industrial knowledge economy, then access to education is important. At the Conservative Party conference in 2012, David Cameron spelled out his theory of why children from poorer backgrounds struggle:

> But isn't the greatest disadvantage of all being written off by those so in hock to a culture of low expectations that they have forgotten what it's like to be ambitious, to want to transcend your background, to overcome circumstance and succeed on your own terms? It's that toxic culture of low expectations – that lack of ambition for every child – which has held this country back.[1]

Echoing Charles Murray, David Cameron placed the emphasis on individuals and the lack of aspiration within poorer communities. For some reason, the Eton- and Oxford-educated prime minister with family connections to the Royal Family couldn't empathise with those who grew up in a different social world to him.

Successive approaches of Conservative and New Labour governments sought to reduce the welfare budget spent on unemployment, even though only 1 per cent of the welfare budget was spent on unemployment benefit in the financial year ending 2017 with most – approximately 42 per cent – spent on pensions.[2] The focus on the media and politicians is rarely placed on this latter aspect of state welfare spending, however.

Tuition fees for university education have also had an impact on the fortunes of the next generation, despite record numbers of students attending university. The next section will show how important having education is for a person's social and economic position in society. What has also changed is the employment context of 21st-century Britain with more people, predominantly young graduates, on short-term, temporary or 'zero-hours' contracts that require flexibility on the part of the employee. Many of these contracts are low paid and insecure, and this contributes to growing social inequalities that, on their current course, are only set to widen in future years.

Social class in 21st-century Britain

Popular categories of class focus on income and profession,[3] drawing on the traditional conception of class as outlined by Weber and Marx. French social theorist Emile Durkheim similarly theorised occupational groups as the basis of a kind of class model, although on a more defined level than Weber and Marx. Rather than the popular notion of three classes, the government has used the Registrar-General's Social Classes (subsequently renamed *Social Class based on Occupation*, or SC) for the census and other analyses since 1913. These divide the population into six groups: professional; managerial and technical; skilled non-manual; skilled manual; partly skilled;

and unskilled. Early sociological analyses drew on this schema, and that of British sociologist John Goldthorpe and colleagues, which introduced a sevenfold classification that introduced new managerial, technical and service sector jobs around the 1970s. As before, this focused on economic position and didn't explicitly take into account the subtleties of gender or race that might affect one's social standing, let alone social contacts or educational opportunities. Class is arguably best studied in relation to other identities. A working-class black mother has an entirely different experience of and take on class compared to a working-class white man. Chapter 5 discusses intersectionality – the study of multiple axes of identity – to understand how identities and oppressions are co-constituted.

In 2011, the BBC launched the Great British Class Survey.[4] This also suggested that there are seven classes. This was based on the work of French sociologist Pierre Bourdieu and included concepts such as economic, social and cultural 'capital'. It sought to account for the varying ways that class has changed through changing education levels and work opportunities. But more importantly, it doesn't just focus on the economic. Class is not just about having money, but having a range of resources that enables an individual to access particular jobs, social spaces and groups. These social and cultural resources are combined with economic capital to determine one's social status. We will look at the work of Pierre Bourdieu to see how it helps provide an opportunity to focus on different aspects of class, before seeing how it was used in the BBC's Great British Class Survey and analysed by British sociologist Mike Savage and colleagues, both for the BBC and in Savage's *Social Class in the 21st Century* (2015).

The French sociologist Pierre Bourdieu noted in *Distinction* (1984) that social elites were not simply financially endowed. They are there because they possess other resources. He identifies three forms of 'capital' that can be used by individuals: economic, social and cultural capital. Economic is the standard unit of measure for class; it refers to how much money we can access. Overwhelmingly, *Distinction* focuses on the cultural aspects of class. Bourdieu noted that 'taste' was an important part of class distinction. This works well in English as class denotes someone's social standing, but also someone's taste. Footballers and reality TV stars are often derided for their lack of taste, despite having high incomes. For Bourdieu cultural capital is the skills, education and taste that give people the access to certain jobs, groups and networks. He observed that certain cultural tastes are seen as highbrow – Culture with a capital 'C'. This predominantly includes the arts, opera, classical music, jazz, literature and theatre. It is largely those with economic capital, however, who have access to highbrow culture. Alongside 'Culture', education is also important. Education helps to impart the cultural knowledge that builds people's cultural capital. But education is a form of cultural capital in its own right as it is the route to certain jobs. When we look at the importance of education, knowledge and technical skills in the post-industrial economy (which we will do in Chapter 7), this form of cultural capital becomes more important.

Social connections are also important. Bourdieu calls this 'social capital'. While US political scientist Robert Putnam argued that social capital was the social networks an individual was engaged within, he was more focused on the macro aspect of social capital and suggested that we are becoming more individual and removed from other groups. In contrast Pierre Bourdieu suggests that social capital is a resource that can be accessed. It is not necessarily about quantity of social networks, but quality. If we were to have a small social circle, but we know them from Eton and Oxford University (like many past UK prime ministers), then this is going to be potentially more advantageous for our social standing than a wide range of football fans from Northumbria. Again, economic capital facilitates this. Having money can allow an individual to go to the 'right' school or university where one can meet key individuals. According to the social mobility foundation The Sutton Trust, private schools students are 55 times more likely to win a place at Oxford or Cambridge than state school students who qualify for free school meals – the most deprived students.[5] Economic capital can also pay for access to certain private members' clubs, sports clubs or leisure activities that open up social networks. This is known as social closure, and is the way in which economically and socially privileged maintain their resources as well as their social status.

Economic, social and cultural capital are intertwined. Economic capital opens up access to the right cultural avenues and social networks. But one needs the right cultural capital in order to successfully interact within social networks and capitalise on the opportunities they may present. It is no good joining the local golf club, having the money to buy all the equipment, but not knowing how to play, let alone having the resources to hold a conversation at the bar afterwards. This is the classic case of 'all the gear and no idea'. Pierre Bourdieu suggested that we embody these different forms of capital. He refers to this as our 'habitus'. It is our manners, attitudes, actions and norms and these reflect our social standing, background and environment. Bourdieu's 'habitus' draws much from the outside, structural factors of an individual. But we also have some choice in how we present ourselves. Through interacting with others, we can determine who we are and how we perform our identity. This is particularly true in a globalised world where there are any number of cultural influences available. What habitus does reflect, however, is the way that we as individuals can immediately feel comfortable – or a complete fish out of water – in a given situation. Through regular repetitive engagement and interaction with a particular group, we can gain the emotional confidence and the social skills to perform the roles correctly.

Pierre Bourdieu's addition of social and cultural capital opens up a new form of analysis away from the traditional upper-, middle- and working-class groupings. Bourdieu added economic and cultural capital onto two axes on a social class matrix. By dissecting social and cultural capital it is possible to divide class into four rough classes. It also shows that class is a spectrum that does not neatly pigeonhole people but indicates a wide range of influences. Those with high cultural and economic capital are often the social elites who like 'high culture', have accessed the best schools and universities, and work in jobs with high incomes. We could divide this into those who like opera, attended Oxbridge, work in the City, are members of the Marylebone Cricket Club and read the *Daily Telegraph*.

Next there are those with high cultural and low economic capital. These will have a university education and like art, culture and literature, read *The Guardian*, but will have less economic capital, like university lecturers. Those with high economic capital and low cultural capital are those with good jobs and savings, but maybe without the education levels. And those with low economic and low cultural capital are those who work in semi-skilled work, read the *Sun* or the *Mirror*, and like football, rock and pop music. While Bourdieu's classification continues to reify 'high culture', it is important to note that his argument was about how those with the resources determine what is taste and what is not. Despite his astute class analysis, Bourdieu's conception of cultural capital is highly racialised, valuing 'white' over 'ethnic' capitals. As British sociologist Katy Sian observes, knowledge of 'Kabaddi, fluency in Urdu, the sounds of Public Enemy, and the poetry of Ruminator wouldn't quite make the cut here!' (Sian 2019: 132).

Pierre Bourdieu's work has influenced many sociologists as they try to make sense of the changing dynamics of British society. The BBC's Great British Class Survey was designed in conjunction with the British sociologist Mike Savage and colleagues in 2013. They used the work of Bourdieu to design a survey that took into account these three concepts and then promoted it widely through the BBC. This provided an opportunity to engage a wide range of the population and assess how Britain has changed. This survey sought to depart from the grand theories of Marx and Weber to better model the contemporary person's position in the social hierarchy. Some argue, however, that this perspective is not necessarily new, simply a reformulation of classic notions of class stratification which attempt to understand social exclusion, albeit based on a more nuanced and culturally informed understanding of social division.

The seven social classes

1. **Elite** This is the wealthiest and most privileged group in the UK. They went to private school and elite universities and enjoy high

cultural activities such as listening to classical music and going to the opera.

2. **Established middle class** This is the most gregarious and the second wealthiest of all the class groups. They work in traditional professions and socialise with a wide variety of people, and take part in a wide variety of cultural activities.

3. **Technical middle class** This is a small, distinctive and prosperous new class group. They prefer emerging culture, such as social media, and mix mainly among themselves. They work in science and tech and come from middle-class backgrounds.

4. **New affluent workers** These people are economically secure, without being well-off. This class group is sociable, has lots of cultural interests and sits in the middle of all the groups in terms of wealth. They're likely to come from working-class backgrounds.

5. **Traditional working class** This group has the oldest average age, and they're likely to own their own home. They mix among themselves and don't enjoy emerging culture. Jobs in this group include lorry drivers, cleaners and electricians.

6. **Emergent service workers** These young people have high social and cultural capital – so they know people from all different walks of life, and enjoy a wide range of cultural activities – but are not financially secure.

7. **Precariat** The poorest and most deprived social group. They tend to mix socially with people like them and don't have a broad range of cultural interests. More than 80 per cent rent their home.

Mike Savage and colleagues divide cultural capital into two areas: high culture and emerging cultural capital. The latter focuses on the new range of cultural lifestyles emerging in contemporary British society. This helps to engage with the demographic changes taking place in the UK. Young people, who predominantly are in the 'emergent service worker' class, engage in a wide range of cultural activities, such as going to festivals, gigs and consuming new music. They just don't tend to engage in high culture like the opera. Reiterating the role of an education in the knowledge economy, those with a degree were in three key social groups: the 'elites', 'established middle class' and 'emergent service worker'. While it is more obvious that those in the established middle class of professionals would have a high proportion of degrees and university education, the fact that the new class of 'emergent service workers' also have a high number of degrees shows how the service sector has grown in significance in the knowledge economy, and that young people are being encouraged to gain an education in order to access the global economy. This also shows how the post-industrial economy has significantly grown a managerial and technical class. Educational attainment is lower within the new affluent workers, who have economic capital and vital manual skills, but ones that don't tend to require a degree. They tend to be male. The 'traditional working class' also has low educational levels and is a shrinking group. They are mainly female and are the oldest group in the survey. To some extent this reiterates how the old class boundaries have changed, and also how gender groups fall across these new categories.

Social capital is also important. This survey disputes the idea that individuals in the lower classes are those who are most socially isolated. The 'technical middle class' is actually the group with the fewest social contacts. While they have high educational levels that allow them access to technological and scientific careers, they do not socialise extensively outside of their own social group. In contrast, the 'emergent service workers' have a wide range of social capital. As they are younger, and more likely to be engaged in social media, they remain in contact with a wider network of people. This class is also more ethnically diverse, and less likely to have had a parent who went to university. This helps to explain their wide range of interest in emerging cultural capital but their relative lack of economic capital.

The 'precariat' is the most impoverished of the seven classes (see Box 4.3). They have low social, economic and cultural capital. This makes it harder for them to materially change their status. They don't have the resources, the social contacts or the money to access the jobs, education or social groups that will enable them to achieve social mobility. The analysis that Bourdieu's theory provides helps us to explain why the 'precariat' will struggle to escape their material situation, rather than by making moral judgements about their family

Box 4.3: The 'precariat': a modern day social class

The term 'precariat' comes from the work of British economist Guy Standing. In *The Precariat: The New Dangerous Class* (2011), Standing suggests that there is a new class of predominantly younger people who are working in low-paid, low-skilled and insecure jobs, predominantly in the service sector such as retail, catering and hospitality. While younger people have often got their first jobs in these areas, there have often been routes out, both within the sector or into other jobs. Standing suggests that the 'precariat' are finding that their access to traditional career ladders is disappearing. As the global economy is focusing on cheap labour, the predominantly young people who make up the 'precariat' have to navigate increasingly more complex job markets. Standing explicitly links the formation of this class as a direct consequence of neoliberal policies over the past 40 years, which have raised job insecurity in order for profit maximisation, at the same time removing state support to protect against this precariousness. He suggests that this class is dangerous because they will form the angry movements that will mobilise politically to challenge the existing global market economy.

situations and then equating this with crime and voluntarily stepping out of the labour market, as per Charles Murray's conceptualisation of the underclass. The 'precariat' are often employed in low-paid, temporary jobs on zero-hours contracts, which makes it much harder for them to escape their situation.

There are subtle differences between the 'precariat' coined by British economist Guy Standing (2011), and the class of the same name in the Great British Class Survey. The employment difficulties are the same for both in that the types of jobs members of this class work in are low-paid, temporary and zero hours. Yet the composition of this class is different based on the cultural and social capital of the members. Many of the members of Standing's 'precariat' are actually the young people found in Savage's 'emergent service workers'. These workers have cultural capital and social contacts that could allow them to change their class at some point in the future. A university education in the knowledge economy is still desirable, even if one is working in the precarious service sector. The members of Savage's 'precariat' don't have access to this education or social networks so will find it much harder to materially change their social status. Consequently, they also find it much harder to mobilise politically in order to challenge their social position. According to the Great British Class Survey, over a third of the British population are 'precariat' and 'emergent service workers'. This is a significant number of people working in low-paid, precarious work, and highlights how the global economy has not raised everybody's opportunities, as Ulrich Beck suggested it would.

These studies also show how income inequality has been increasing since the 1970s. It is also being concentrated in the hands of a smaller group of people. The 'elite' are concentrated around London where they not only have the economic capital to live in the country's capital, but also the economic resources to use the amenities that the city provides. We will see how this links back to the analysis of Dutch sociologist Saskia Sassen in Chapter 7. Global cities concentrate economic resources for the elites, while dispersing cheap labour across the globe. This process of concentration and dispersal helps account for the small number of elites in London and the growing precariat across the country. However, Sassen may have begun to theorise the demise of the elite. The furore over the UK leaving the EU has contributed to increasing ill feeling towards the UK political elite, in particular, as reckless and self-serving. It is yet to be seen what implications this will have for the future of class relations in the UK.

KEY POINTS SUMMARY

- Karl Marx and Max Weber are seen as the pioneers of traditional class analysis, which tends to see wealth and occupation as the key determinants of social class position.
- French sociologist Bourdieu theorised the cultural dimensions of class and ushered in a new type of cultural analysis which saw cultural and social capital as key to social mobility and class reproduction.
- More recent class analysis has conceptualised classes beyond the traditional upper-, middle- and working-class categories, considering lifestyle and cultural consumption, as well as occupation and wealth.
- The elite in society tend to capitalise on and restrict access to the wealth and opportunities that have come as a result of the growth of the global economy, which has seen income inequality worsen in the age of globalisation.
- The criminalisation and scapegoating of certain social groups in society framed as the 'underclass' allows the political elite to reframe structural issues of inequality as personal and cultural failings.

KEY READING GUIDE

- *The Communist Manifesto*, written by by Karl Marx and Friedrich Engels and published as a political pamphlet in 1848, lays out one of the seminal political ideologies of all time and is illustrative of Marx's historically informed theory of class struggle.
- Guy Standing's *The Precariat: The New Dangerous Class* (2011) gives a solid introduction to a growing section of society that is economically unstable and increasingly politically discontent.
- In *Chavs: The Demonisation of the Working Class* (2011), journalist and political campaigner Owen Jones takes aim at middle -class contempt for the working classes by discussing the framing of the UK underclass through the 'chav'.

- Beverley Skeggs, in *Formations of Class and Gender* (1997) and *Class, Self and Culture* (2004), looks at the experiences of working-class women, and the way class acts as a form of value and self-worth for individuals and communities.
- In *Racism, Class and The Racialized Outsider* (2014), Satnam Virdee puts an understanding of racism and nationalism at the centre of his class analysis. This book will help you bring together ideas from Chapters 3 and 4, to understand how the racial hierarchy and the class hierarchy are co-constituted.

Notes

[1] www.newstatesman.com/blogs/politics/2012/10/david-camerons-speech-conservative-conference-full-text
[2] www.ons.gov.uk/economy/governmentpublicsectorandtaxes/publicsectorfinance/articles/howisthewelfarebudgetspent/2016-03-16
[3] www.ons.gov.uk/methodology/classificationsandstandards/otherclassifications/thenationalstatisticssocioeconomicclassificationnssecrebasedonsoc2010
[4] Its online calculator is available at www.bbc.com/news/magazine-22000973
[5] www.suttontrust.com/newsarchive/private-school-pupils-55-times-likely-go-oxbridge-poor-students/

5

Gender

One of the major critiques of sociology is that there is too great a focus on the 'founding fathers' of sociology, namely Emile Durkheim, Karl Marx and Max Weber. Although there are some prominent early female writers, like Harriet Martineau from Britain and Jane Adams from the US, early writings are predominately written by men, about men and for men. They wrote about the male experience and did not really take into account differences based on gender. If you go back and look at the earlier quotes by these theorists, they all use 'he', 'him', or 'man' as a shorthand for 'he or she', 'him or her', or 'human'. They didn't consider that the non-male experience could be different. Thus, the 'dead white men' approach to social theory has been heavily critiqued in recent years. The success of feminism is therefore that it has not just brought about legislative and cultural changes in wider society, but it has centralised gender as an analytical tool so we can understand society through different perspectives. As with race and class, it is important to listen to the lived experience of people, not to assume that their experience is the same as ours.

This chapter addresses the dominant position men and masculinity have taken in society. It then outlines how there have been broadly three 'waves' of feminism in the West. The first wave centred on the right to vote and basic property rights at the start of the 20th century. Equal access to the workplace and education, and control of reproductive rights became the focus of the second wave in the 1960s. By the 1980s the third wave understood women's experiences to be varied depending on many factors, particularly class, ethnicity and sexuality. This is followed by a discussion of transgender and how it challenges and reaffirms our understandings of gender. The varied dimensions of gender are then outlined in a section on intersectionality, which addresses the intersections of gender with class and race.

One of the many important things about feminism is how it challenges the core of our assumptions about society. Feminists have sought to make 'the personal political'. Everyday life becomes a space to challenge inequality. Social media feeds like #everydaysexism provide a space for women and men to challenge misogyny and sexism that takes place in small ways. These 'microaggressions' can build up over time to show how we still live in a society that is heavily structured around gender. Chapters 3 and 4 on class and race reiterate a common theme: while there was some acknowledgement of inequalities in the past, particularly until the 1970s, legislation and changing cultural attitudes indicates that those inequalities have all but disappeared. Just as politicians and commentators suggest that we are in a post-racial world, or that 'we are all middle class', others suggest that we are in a post-feminist society where gender inequality is a thing of the past. In contrast, British cultural theorist Angela McRobbie (2009) argues in relation to feminism that there is a simultaneous culture of female empowerment at the same time as an entrenching of traditional gender norms.

The key thing to emphasise in the study of the sociology of gender is the difference between sex and gender. In *Sex, Gender and Society* (1972) British sociologist Ann Oakley makes a distinction with sex being the anatomical and physiological, which signify biological male and femaleness. Gender, meanwhile, is the socially constructed norms of masculinity and femininity. US anthropologist Gayle Rubin (1975) adds sexuality to this definition and makes gender distinct from biological reproduction. Gender, Rubin (1975: 179) argues, is a 'socially imposed division of the sexes'. Gender is about the suppression of differences and emphasising differences. This is how we 'see' male and female in society, because what usually denotes being male or female – our genitalia – aren't usually on public display. In this way, certain social markers come to symbolise men and women. Body hair is seen as male so women take great pains (literally) to have hair removed, not just on the face, but across their bodies. These socially enforced norms can even be seen in consumer goods. The British comedian Bridget Christie highlighted how Bic, the pen manufacturer, made a 'Bic for Her' because women obviously can't use ordinary biros or pens. 'I expect', said Christie, 'that's why the Brontës were so shit at writing' (Nicholson, 2013).

Hegemonic masculinity

We can see how gender becomes essentialised through masculinity. There is a popular image of the so-called 'alpha male'; the confident, physically and emotionally strong, (hetero)sexually active male. Historically, these attributes have been privileged and this has excluded women and men who do not conform. What this shows, however, is that gender is partially relative. We perform it in relation to others, both other men and other women. But there are also plurals. There is not a pure masculinity or femininity, but masculinities and femininities. As shown elsewhere in the book, we have multiple identities and these are shaped by our sense of self in relation to the social world around us and the sorts of social situations we find ourselves in. In this sense, we act male or female depending on our audience. Popular assumptions about masculinity and femininity focused on heterosexuality. This approach is what we term 'heteronormative': the norm is to be heterosexual. As influential Jamaican-British cultural theorist Stuart Hall noted (1996), identity is often determined by our differences from others. In this way masculinity is reflected as not being feminine. It is seen as being straight and physically and emotionally tough. This implies that to be gay, emotional, or less physically strong is seen as feminine. When we discuss the importance of feminism later, these 'masculine' traits can become problematic for women who are not seen as 'feminine'.

To reinforce the performance aspect of gender, we can return to another contemporary phenomenon: trolling. Often social media trolls use gender-based abuse to emphasise their supposed superiority. Again, sociology helps explain. If these men are naturally superior, then why do they need to resort to abuse? Nature would take its course and these men would 'naturally' rise to the top. Yet gender is not solely based on nature. It is socially constructed and many young men, particularly working-class men, feel sidelined by the new global economy. As shown throughout this book, there has been a significant shift in how the global economy operates and what skills are required in contemporary Britain. The knowledge economy requires university level education, often in areas that need technical skills like computing or engineering, or in the service sector. The traditional attributes of young men being confident, physical and anti-academic are not necessarily successful in the new global economy. This is not to say that certain masculine traits are not still privileged. As shown in Chapter 4, the class of 'new affluent workers' is predominantly male. This class is comprised of semi-skilled manual workers who have successfully carved a career in building, electrical work, plumbing and logistics. Outside this, men are still more likely to dominate senior positions in corporations and the gender pay gap remains woefully large despite over 40 years of equal pay legislation. Figure 5.1 shows that a gender pay gap persists across all occupational types, for both part-time and full-time female workers. It is most prominent in traditionally male occupations like the skilled trades, but still exists in female dominated sectors like customer service and care work. However, in professional and managerial occupations there is also a significant gap. This is larger for part-time than full-time workers in professional occupations, even though women tend to take up part-time positions more so than men: part-time female professionals earn over 20 per cent less on average than part-time male professionals (the glass ceiling, see Box 5.1, ensures that there are also far fewer female professionals overall than men). Equal Pay Day is held each year in November as the symbolic day when women effectively work for free until the end of the year.

Figure 5.1: Mean UK full-time and part-time gender pay gap figures, 2018

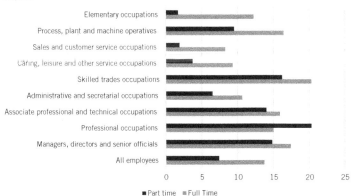

Note: The gender pay gap is defined as the average difference between men's and women's hourly earnings as a percentage of men's earnings.

Source: Annual Survey of Hours and Earnings, Office for National Statistics licensed under the Open Government Licence v.1.0, UK, www.ons.gov.uk/employmentandlabourmarket/peopleinwork/earningsandworkinghours/datasets/annualsurveyofhoursandearningsashegenderpaygaptables

Gendered behaviours are learned from the social world around us. Often these are learned in school and the home. In *Learning to Labour: How Working Class Kids get Working Class Jobs* (1977) British sociologist Paul Willis showed how we learn from an early age what types of jobs we think we can apply for and what behaviours are required. Boys in particular learn not to be seen as too clever as this isn't the way that men should be. They are expected to play sports, chase girls and be physically aggressive. The British comedian Micky Flanagan (2009) has used this observation in his comedy. He observed that at school in the East End of London in the 1970s, the careers adviser came and asked everyone what he or she wanted to do when they left school. It turned out that the most ambitious kid in the school was Gary who wanted to drive a van. Flanagan and his mates laughed at Gary for being a dreamer. No kid from their school went on to drive a van; their school was there to produce the people that carry stuff *to* the van. Certainly, Willis' work is overly focused on men and boys, but does highlight how certain class and gendered assumptions are made.

Box 5.1: The persistence of the glass ceiling

The concept of the glass ceiling represents the invisible barriers that keep not only women but the working classes and minority ethnic groups out of certain industries and senior levels of authority and management. There is a myriad of reasons as to why women specifically are underrepresented at these levels. Gender discrimination is regarded to be the primary reason, couched not only in unconscious biases against women but the lack of family-friendly policies that allow women (and men) to work more flexibly. The fact that the burdens of childcare and domestic labour still fall disproportionately on women means demanding jobs are simply not feasible routes for many women. Masculine work cultures where 'laddish' behaviour and over-confidence is rewarded and sexual harassment is often overlooked also account for the lack of presence of women in industries such as finance. Facebook Chief Operating Office Sheryl Sandberg's urge to women to 'lean in' at work – in a nutshell, to be more assertive – underestimated the extent to which further structural and cultural change is needed before women are truly on an even playing field with men.

One way of developing our sociological imagination around gender is through analysing the privileging of certain traits, attributes and behaviours. Australian sociologist Raewyn Connell (1987, 1995) discusses the concept of 'hegemonic masculinity'. She draws on the work of Italian Marxist philosopher Antonio Gramsci (1971) who identifies the power dynamic operating within wider culture that ensures certain social elites remain in power. This power dynamic was called 'hegemony'. Similarly, Pierre Bourdieu showed that certain forms of cultural capital (in particular) are seen as culturally important which enables individuals and groups to access the social elites (we covered that in detail in Chapter 4). With 'hegemonic masculinity', Connell observes that the characteristics of the 'alpha male' have been privileged. These behaviours become self-reproducing as (predominantly) men who exhibit these actions push themselves to into positions of power through, in part, the marginalisation and dominance (see Box 5.2) of women, and of men who do not embody and perform traditional gender norms.

Privileging certain forms of (predominantly) gendered behaviour isn't necessarily something explicit and political, but can be unconscious. Psychologists have observed cognitive bias in our interactions since the 1970s. More recently, studies have looked at specific forms of unconscious bias, particularly towards gender and ethnicity. In *Orchestrating Impartiality*, US economists Claudia Goldin and Cecilia Rouse (2000) conducted an analysis that addressed the predominance of male musicians in orchestras. One would think that musical ability would be the prime focus for musical directors. Yet in the 1970s only 5 per cent of musicians were female. The musical director would handpick the musicians, usually those who had been

Box 5.2: The rise of the #MeToo movement

Sparked in part by the sexual assault allegations against US film producer Harvey Weinstein, the #MeToo movement took off on Twitter in 2017 with women, particularly actresses, sharing their common experiences of sexual harassment in the workplace. The phrase 'Me Too' was coined years earlier by social activist Tarana Burke, as a way for women – particularly women of colour – to expose the extent of sexual harassment and abuse against them. The movement has spread from the arts to academia, sports, politics and finance and has prompted an examination of the levels of diversity and equality across industries, as well as the extent to which employers and companies across the world are taking sexual harassment seriously.

trained by well-respected teachers. With gender equality legislation, jobs were advertised more widely, but the gender discrepancy remained. One factor that did affect the gender balance within the orchestra was the implementation of 'blind auditions'. During auditions, musicians were given numbers, rather than names, screens were installed, and even the floor softened so that footsteps could not be detected. Goldin and Rouse found that with blind auditions, female musicians were 50 per cent more likely to be hired. Musical directors were not explicitly biased towards men, but unconsciously following people like them. This shows how ingrained gendered norms are in both society and our own psyches.

We can see hegemonic masculinity exhibited in schools and universities across the country. This 'Lad culture' manifests itself in a specific performance of masculinity, predominantly through excessive drinking and sexual harassment. Lad culture emerged with *Playboy* magazine in the 1950s, but re-entered popular culture in the 1990s with 'lads' mags' like *Loaded* and *Nuts*. The editorial staples of these magazines were semi-naked women, sport and humorous articles, mainly around drinking and drugs. The internet and social media manifestations of this culture can be found with Uni Lad and the Lad Bible. Sex, football and alcohol became the 'holy trinity' of lad culture. As our identities are a social performance, this form of hegemonic masculinity can be performed through the consumption of all three.

Online, lad culture proves to be even more insidious. There has been a convergence of the alt-right and 'men's rights' activists in recent years. Online and social media platforms allow these individuals anonymity and access to a likeminded community through which to voice outright and often vitriolic misogyny, racisms, homophobia and general discontent with progressive, inclusive social movements. These 'activists' are akin to 'incels' – members of the 'involuntary celibate online subculture' – in that they believe women and the feminist movement are to blame for a whole host of social ills, but particularly the lack of attention they believe they receive from the opposite sex.

'Lad culture' has increasingly hit the headlines through its aggressive sexualised and violent expression of power on university campuses. According to research by the National Union of Students, lad culture is particularly prevalent in the social side of university – extracurricular activities, sports and nights out – as well as in the way certain gender-related subjects taught and discussed at university, increasingly in the mainstream, are negatively characterised. In the National Union of Students (NUS) study 'That's What She Said' commissioned in 2012 – the first major study into lad culture at universities – 50 per cent of participants identified a prevailing sense of sexism in and around campuses.[1] Although lad culture is prevalent across most social spaces and affects men as well as women, young as well as old, female students are particularly at risk. Revolt Sexual Assault, a national campaign working to expose the extent of sexual harassment experienced by students at UK universities, stated that 48 per cent of female students and recent graduates they surveyed in 2017 and 2018 have experienced sexual assault, and 8 per cent of female students reported having been raped while at university in comparison to an estimated 4 per cent of the female population at large.[2]

Lad culture is also a reflection of the growing neoliberalisation of society. British sociologists Alison Phipps and Isabel Young in *Neoliberalisation and 'Lad Cultures' in Higher Education* (2015) suggest that as individuals are being turned into consumers, they are increasingly providing feedback to organisations, rating their meal, hotel or flight through Tripadvisor or on social media. Within universities there is the National Student Survey, with regular monitoring of student satisfaction throughout the academic course. Phipps and Young note that sexual competition has long been a privileged form of hegemonic masculinity. Women, particularly as sexual objects, are rated and objectified within this broader culture. Facebook has pages labelled 'Rate your Shag' and groups of lads openly declare how sexually attractive they think women are. In some cases, this leads to physical, psychological and sexual intimidation.

There is some suggestion that 'lad culture' is a defensive response to a 'crisis of masculinity'. The narrative goes that men are being excluded due to women's relative success within the labour market. As women have entered the workplace, men have been displaced. The British geographer Linda McDowell (2000) argues that the 'crisis of masculinity' has roots in the restructuring of the global economy, as well as complex intersections of class and ethnicity, and changing understandings of masculinity. Paul Willis' (1977) young men knew that they could get working-class jobs, so saw school as irrelevant. This doesn't work in the new global economy and boys are finding it harder to adapt. As noted throughout this book, the informational economy privileges university education in the workplace, and it is women who are now surpassing men in academic achievement. Young men who feel excluded from the labour market cling to traditional forms of hegemonic masculinity that are no longer tolerated in the modern workplace. In a global and more gender-neutral working environment we are expected to be 'other directed', as David Riesman observed. We can no longer rely on traditional forms of behaviour, but have to adjust and adapt out values and be in constant change.

When we acknowledge that gender is socially determined by wider social factors then it becomes possible to subvert and challenge dominant forms of masculinity. As Connell stated, hegemonic masculinity privileges a small number of men who exhibit certain behaviour traits, like confidence, physical and emotional strength. When we privilege this type of masculinity it excludes not only women, but also other forms of masculinity. For this reason it is important that men help challenge gender inequality because it only benefits certain men. The gender pay gap may relatively privilege men over women, but this means that employers are suppressing wages to women and using this power dynamic to ultimately keep wages lower for men, except those men (and few women) who can break into the elite tiers of business or politics. The 'HeForShe' campaign set up by UN Women and launched by the actor Emma Watson in 2014, reiterates the importance of men to engage with feminism and act as agents of change.

The importance of feminism

In *The Second Sex* (1949), French feminist Simone de Beauvoir made a clear case that women have historically been seen as second-class citizens. She argued that women have consistently been judged based on their bodies, both external image and perceived physical weaknesses. *The Second Sex* is seen as the start of 'second wave feminism'. The 'first wave' occurred during the 19th and early 20th centuries and primarily focused on access to the state. Earlier 18th and 19th century thinkers like Mary Wollstonecraft drew on other Enlightenment thinkers to argue that there were not just universal rights of men, but rights of women too. Female suffrage was a key part of the wider debates around parliamentary reform and campaign for workers' rights that resulted from the rapid urbanisation and industrialisation throughout the 19th century. Women across the world were fighting for the right to vote (or suffrage) at this time. In Britain, the label of 'suffragettes' was attached to the women of the Women's Social and Political Union who took a wide range of direct action in order to raise the issue in the public imagination. From coordinated arson attacks to hunger strikes, the suffragettes campaigned to have the right to vote. This was eventually granted in 1918 for women over 30 who met certain property rights or marriage status. It has now been over 100 years since British women were first able to vote in general elections. All men over 21 were also given the vote for the first time. The property rights reinforced how this movement was predominantly a white middle-class movement. But it also highlighted how women were still considered to be part of a man's social unit, rather than independent in their own right.

With 'second wave' feminism, feminists sought to celebrate and exemplify the qualities of women in famous 'second wave' books like Betty Friedan's 1963 *The Feminine Mystique* and *The Female Eunuch* by Germaine Greer in 1970. The former exploded the myth of the happy suburban middle-class housewife. Friedan called for women to ask themselves what they truly wanted, rather than being subservient to the social norms of marriage and the nuclear family. Greer focused on female sexuality and confronted the 'sense of inferiority or natural dependence' that women felt obliged to accept passively.

Many of the writings of 'second wave' feminists were culturally significant. They influenced many women (and some men). They were not restricted to universities or political groups, but were part of a much wider movement. These ideas sprang from the civil rights, student, anti-war, and more obviously, the women's liberation movements. Throughout the 1960s and 1970s these movements challenged the established (hegemonic) view of the society. Women's liberation consistently fought against the oppression of women as well as fighting for greater equality. Women's bodies became one of the central battlegrounds. Part of this fight was through control of their own reproductive rights, which still continues today over the right to abortions, contraception and adequate healthcare.

The expectation of women to have slim beautiful bodies is the other key feminist battleground. The fashion industry and media consistently present women as sexualised objects to be consumed by the 'male gaze'. Women are portrayed as passive objects, often scantily clad in order to elicit a sexualised response. When men are photographed, they are often fully clothed. If semi-clothed or naked, men will still be in assertive poses, often looking confidently into the camera. Women are often depicted as accessories to men, draped over his arm or looking at him, while he looks at the camera. There has been an ongoing discussion, particularly within the music industry, about whether the culture of sexualisation represents female liberation and legitimate artistic expression, or objectification. 'Self' sexualisation arguably suggests that women are no longer solely the object of the male gaze, but have the opportunity and autonomy to present themselves as they want. The sort of social messages emitted are potentially harmful, however. Particularly so when corporations as opposed to music artists are the culprits. In the summer of 2015, an advert for a weight loss supplement depicted a toned blonde woman in a yellow bikini and asked the question 'are you beach body ready?'. The implication was that only those with slim and toned bodies are permitted on the beach. These images exert immeasurable pressure on women to conform to an ideal. In *Fat is a Feminist Issue* (1981),

British psychologist Susie Orbach observed how this pressure led to a prevalence of eating disorders among women as they seek to assert some control over their own bodies. Women are also pressured not to have muscular bodies as these are seen as overly masculine. Female athletes and bodybuilders are consistently challenged to demonstrate their femininity through fashion, long hair and make-up. These cases reinforce how our sense of self and our bodies are shaped by wider social world.

Rather than gender being a 'natural' or 'biological' certainty, gender is a continually performed part of our identity. 'Third wave' feminism began to question to absolute and essentialised arguments of the 'second wave'. As outlined in Chapter 3 our identity is a regularly performed act. In this sense it is 'performative': we perform our identity. US philosopher Judith Butler noted that this helps to distinguish between biological sex and sociological gender. She argued that gender is performed regularly and we take our understanding of gender from the social world around us – 'There is no "doer behind the deed", but that the "doer" is variably constructed in and through the deed' (Butler, 1990: 142). By wearing certain clothes, carrying our bodies in certain ways and undertaking certain activities, then we perform our gender to others. There are certain cultural markers that denote gender. Wearing a dress or skirt suggests in European culture that the wearer is female. Likewise, make-up, long eyelashes and painted fingernails also denote 'femininity'. As Bourdieu noted in Chapter 4, we embody our cultural capital through our habitus. If we regularly play rugby then our body shape reflects this. If we have given birth then the body changes. Butler noted that gender could be subverted through drag. She argued that this reiterated the gender norms as male drag artists explicitly use female signifiers within this subversion, and vice versa.

The transgender movement

Transgenderism highlights the performativity of gender. Highly public transgender personalities, such as Caitlyn Jenner, Chelsea Manning and Kellie Maloney, placed the role of transgender

Figure 5.2: The Drag Kings of Manchester at the Manchester Gay Pride Parade, 2012

prominently in the public eye. Transgender highlights the distinction between sex and gender. Many 'second wave' feminists do not recognise this distinction, and therefore do not recognise transgender identities, some to a greater degree of intensity than others (see Box 5.3). In October 2015, Germaine Greer was 'no-platformed' by students at Cardiff University because she publicly stated that postoperative transwomen were not female. Transgendered identity highlights how gendered behaviour is learned and performed. How does someone tell the world that they are a different gender except through the clothes and make-up that defines gender socially?

One of the classic studies of transgender was presented by US sociologist Harold Garfinkel in his *Studies in Ethnomethodology* (1967). Garfinkel's approach was to highlight the everyday actions and 'common sense' assumptions we make. His 'breaching experiments' would force people to confront their assumptions. For example,

Box 5.3: TERFS

The acronym 'TERF' stands for 'trans-exclusionary radical feminist'. Some feminists claim that transgender and transsexual people uphold sexist gender roles and binaries which are antithetical to the feminist project. The term TERF has thus been used – derogatorily – to describe those who believe that trans women can never really be women, and/or cannot empathise with the sort of oppressions experienced by women born female. The fact of the matter is – as per intersectionality – that every woman's experience of being a woman is different, and trans women face their own unique and debilitating set of discriminations. Trans-inclusive feminists like US radical feminist Catherine Mackinnon support trans people's right to self-identification, stating that anyone who identifies as a woman and wants to be a woman is a woman.

when people walk into a lift, they turn in and face the centre or the door. We don't stand and face the wall. Yet if someone were to do that, other people would view that person as unusual or odd. These mundane, everyday actions reveal how we think, act and interact with others. Comedy characters like Borat, as played by Sacha Baron Cohen (2006), undertake similar 'breaching experiments' for comic effect. One of Garfinkel's (1967) case studies was of Agnes, a woman who was raised as a boy until she was 17 and moved away from home. This gave her the opportunity to live as a woman because she was able to present herself to strangers who had no knowledge of her backstory. This provided some difficulties, as she didn't have the social resources to draw on when meeting people. But it also revealed how she too learned to put on make-up, what clothes to wear, how to walk, and how to 'act' female. Gender, like other forms of identity, is intrinsically performative.

Intersectionality

A central theme of this book is that social life is intricately connected. Our sociological imagination helps us to make the links to other everyday aspects of our social lives. This is particularly true of gender. Women and men are not hermetically sealed entities, but influenced by many different parts of our identities. They are also influenced by different social factors, such as our class, ethnicity and sexuality. How these influences 'intersect' affects individuals depending on the context. The term 'intersectionality' ensures that these different factors are taken into account. First and second wave feminism were often centred on white middle-class women who had the cultural and social capital to challenge the social world around them. This is not to minimise their achievements, but social inequalities are not uniform for everyone. Growing up as a poor working-class white woman is different from growing up as the daughter of Barack and Michelle Obama. White women in the UK live their gender through their social class. Asian and black women live their gender through their gender, *class* and ethnicity. Their femininity is constructed from a more constrained expectation of what it means to be female. US theorist bell hooks argued that feminism was racist in *Feminist Theory: From Margin to Centre* (1984). hooks stated that feminist discussions did not take into account the various forms of inequality in US society and that oppression comes from racial and economic inequality as well. In *Black Feminist Thought* (1990), US sociologist Patricia Hill Collins clearly argues for these distinctions to be made clear. She suggests that black women are the 'outsider-within'. In the US, they have often been involved in domestic duties within the home, but were not considered part of the family. Within feminist circles, black women are outside as feminism has historically been focused on white middle-class women.

As noted in Chapter 4, intersectionality is the study of the transformative effect that class, gender, race, sexuality and disability have on people's identities, and the sorts of marginalisation and inequality different sub-groups may experience in society. The origins of intersectionality lie in the US black female intellectual tradition which sought to draw attention to how the experience of women is shaped by race and class. The term was coined by Kimberlé Crenshawe, a US scholar in the field of critical race theory, who sought to construct a lens through which the intersection of power – particularly through maleness and whiteness – could be understood. Feminist thought from the 1970s onwards adopted a universalising rhetoric of gender which claimed to embrace all women but really only considered the experience of middle-class white women in North America or Western Europe. For women of colour, these perspectives didn't take into account their gendered position within their specific racial communities, or their racial position within larger society and within the larger female population. Intersectional feminist Flavia Dzodan created the catchphrase 'My feminism will be intersectional or it will be bullshit!' in response to the way she believes white feminists allow racism pass unchallenged when solely promoting gender equality. As we have stressed throughout this book, it is vital to understand that each person sees and experiences the world in different ways. The sort of political agendas advanced by civil rights activists or by Western feminists didn't take into account the standpoint of people of colour (see Box 5.4). Intersectionality opened a space for discussion as well as the beginning of legal and political acknowledgement of the unique oppressions felt by those claiming membership of multiple subordinated social groups.

As with anti-racism, a consistent argument levelled at those fighting for gender equality is that thanks to anti-sexist legislation there is no longer gender-based discrimination. As we have seen earlier, there is a political argument that we live in a post-class, post-race and post-gender world. In the neoliberal world of individualised approaches then everyone is free to succeed free of regulation. Despite anti-discrimination legislation, social inequalities continue to persist. For British sociologist Angela McRobbie in *The Aftermath of Feminism* (2009: 11), post-feminism is

a process by which feminist gains of the 1970s and 1980s are actively and relentlessly undermined … through an array of machinations, elements of contemporary popular culture are perniciously effective in regard to this undoing of feminism, while simultaneously appearing to be engaging in a well-informed and even well-intended responses to feminism.

Box 5.4: Alice Goffman's *On the Run*

Intersectionality also puts the spotlight on the researcher and their ability to see through the eyes of others who may, on many axes, radically differ in terms of identity and lived experience from them. *On the Run: Fugitive Life in an American City* began as an ethnographic, immersive research project, later to be a thesis and book (2014), undertaken by US sociologist Alice Goffman in a disadvantaged neighbourhood of Philadelphia. She – a middle-class white academic – observed and analysed young African-American men who were mistreated and targeted by the police, highlighting how the treatment of poor, black people by the criminal justice system affects the lives of families, neighbourhoods and communities. The study has been the source of much controversy, however, centred around the standpoint of researchers in relation to their research 'subjects'.

Popular culture and politicians will talk of women and girls being empowered and liberated, and yet decry them for stepping outside perceived gender conventions. The sidebar of shame on the *Daily Mail's* website featuring candid 'nip slips' and 'side boob' shots of celebrities is testament to how women are viewed and discussed. McRobbie (2009) highlights how there is a 'double movement' where there is simultaneously a liberalisation around certain legal rights around gender and sexuality, and an entrenchment of gender inequalities. Despite the great strides over the past 40 years, women are still more likely to be marginalised in the workplace. Men are still more likely to be in senior positions in business, politics and public institutions, despite the UK having had two female prime ministers in the past 40 years. While overt sexism has declined, microaggressions and subtle forms of discrimination take place. Social media like #everydaysexism highlight how sexist comments persist in contemporary Britain. More importantly, they highlight how these microaggressions, while seemingly small, are repetitive. Just as gender and identity are repetitive acts, sexism and other forms of discrimination are repetitive actions. Each one reinforces that women are, in the words of de Beauvoir, the second sex.

Sociology also shows how other factors are related to gender inequality. Class and race are also significant determinants of achievement. As we saw earlier, working-class boys are also likely to be marginalised in the new global economy as the attributes prized among these groups are not valuable in the knowledge economy. Likewise, traits that are seen as 'feminine', such as quiet, unassertive and modest, don't necessarily ensure success in the higher echelons of institutions. Men are still underrepresented in the so-called caring professions like nursing, but women are underrepresented in science and engineering. Women of colour especially are marginalised and underrepresented in most professional, managerial and technical sectors. The broader social image of these roles is based on gender and we learn that it is not for the likes of us. But as we can see from identity and gender, we can subvert, but it takes a clear confidence that we know this is what we want because the microaggressions can build up and reinforce the differences.

KEY POINTS SUMMARY

- Hegemonic masculinity has a detrimental effect on men and women, by normalising and reinforcing traditionally 'masculine' behaviours which often marginalise and hurt women and men who deviate from these social standards.
- Women are still underpaid in relation to men and underrepresented in relation to men in almost all sectors, despite years of gender equality legislation and campaigning.
- Gender is performative, the repetition of acts and behaviours which entrench and perpetuate cultural gender norms and

binaries. Sex, as well as gender, is also a socially constructed category.

- Intersectionality acknowledges that power and oppression work across multiple axes. Class, race, gender, sexuality and disability work together to marginalise groups and individuals in complex and different ways.

KEY READING GUIDE

- In *Gender Trouble: Feminism and the Subversion of Identity* (1990) Judith Butler introduces the idea of gender and performativity. She deconstructs the idea of 'woman' and 'women', and destabilises the distinction between sex and gender.
- *Women, Race and Class* (1981) by Angela Davis is a classic critical feminist text, giving a thorough grounding in intersectionality and an overview of the development of black feminisms in the US.
- Angela McRobbie critiques the post-feminist shift in *The Aftermath of Feminism: Gender Culture, and Social Change* (2008) which champions female empowerment but works within consumer culture (think: 'makeover' reality television), giving the illusion but not the reality of female autonomy.
- In *Masculinities* (1995) Raewyn W. Connell looks at masculine identity and power and its role in societal gender relations. He analyses the varying levels to which men construct and uphold hegemonic masculinities, and the concurrent effect on both men and women.

Notes

[1] www.nus.org.uk/Global/Campaigns/That's%20what%20she%20 said%20full%20report%20Final%20web.pdf.

[2] https://revoltsexualassault.com/wp-content/uploads/2018/03/Report-Sexual-Violence-at-University-Revolt-Sexual-Assault-The-Student-Room-March-2018.pdf.

6

Relationships and intimacy

In a country which politicians had claimed was 'classless', the wedding between Prince Harry and Meghan Markle was all about class. The Prince was not only marrying someone from outside the revered bloodlines of European royalty, but also from outside Europe. Markle is a divorced, mixed-race, self-made US woman who proudly calls herself a feminist. As an actor, lifestyle blogger and now Duchess of Sussex, she has provided a platform for women to share their voices, as well as being a vocal champion of the #MeToo movement. British newspapers and magazines enthusiastically reported on her wearing a trouser suit, showing that she would not be officially dressed by the Royal courtiers. This challenges the conservative image of the British Royal Family with its centuries of protocols and customs. Although this provided an exhilarating prospect for the notoriously excitable British media, other features of Markle's life added to the spicy narrative. The sermon after the wedding was given by a black American bishop, followed by gospel singers, which meant it significantly differed from previous royal weddings. Leading up to the event in 2018, the media were full of stories about her estranged father who was not invited to the wedding. Markle's parents divorced when she was a child, and she had a difficult relationship with her father. Since the relationship with Harry was made public, she became a regular news story for the press, and received extensive negative coverage. There was a strong analogy to Harry's mother, Princess Diana, who divorced Prince Charles and died after being chased by paparazzi photographers. In one highly public family, it is possible to see the wider changes to families and relationships in the UK.

Rather than simply looking at the hidden social relations that underpin society, this chapter takes a look at actual relationships. How we form families, friendships, sexual relationships and other forms of intimate relationships is a product of wider society and power relations. In particular, gendered power dynamics permeate many of our social relationships, particularly heterosexual ones. Other forms of sexuality, including gay, lesbian, bisexual and asexual, all challenge dominant social norms and help us to understand society better. Even unpicking the difference between intimacy, love and sex can help us understand why many people are moving away from romantic ideals about finding one person for the rest of our lives. Many may look to fairy-tale weddings of princes and princesses, but the reality for many people is vastly different.

Post-war Britain had fairly stable communities as jobs were kept in the locality, meaning fairly limited internal migration occurred. The idea of stability was reflected in the institution of the family. It also reflected the gendered division of labour of the time. The idyllic ideal of the nuclear family originated during the post-war period as stable employment for men ensured that they provided for a family, while the wife tended to the children. Yet this helped make the labour of housewives invisible, as the British sociologist Anne Oakley argued (1974). As women fought for, and won, significant legislative rights and equalities, the nuclear family began to change. Working mothers challenged the gendered division of labour in the home. Reproductive rights gave women more control over when and whether they had children. The introduction of the Divorce Reform Act in 1969 saw the loosening of the image of the marriage 'til death do us part'. And with growing awareness of gender equality, more women now file for divorce. And the restructuring of the economy led to greater demands on working households, particularly as jobs moved. When individuals or families moved for work, the stable support structures became stretched or disappeared, which further affected the nuclear family. While the 'traditional' nuclear family still exists in some cases, with gender and sexuality equality, the contemporary British family is much more diverse.

Relationships

The classic post-war view of relationships revolved around the image of the nuclear family. This heterosexual unit comprised of a husband, wife and children. The economic division of labour was one of the male breadwinner, and a female housewife and mother. We can see the spatial division here as well. The masculine realm was in public, while women were expected to look after the private sphere. The US sociologist Talcott Parsons, who took a very structured view of society, reified this image. Parsons' theory came to be known as 'functionalism' and viewed society as one large structure with everyone having specific roles to keep society functioning. The nuclear family had a key function within this social system. In *Family, Socialization and Interaction Process* (1955), Parsons highlights the importance of the nuclear family for the success of industrial society. Rather than the broad extended families that have existed throughout history, the nuclear family was smaller. It was free to move as the needs of the economy required. The smaller unit also provided the care environment that industrial society needed. Clearly Parsons ignored other sexualities in privileging the heterosexual nuclear family. He also ignored the inherent gender inequality on which the nuclear family rests. For this stable family unit to function it needs the unpaid labour of women to raise children and do housework. It also relies on a stable economic approach. Chapter 7 shows that the global economy is post-industrial and requires a different type of workforce. Even with a nuclear family, workers are expected to be mobile and free to move to the larger cities, or globally, in order to find work.

While the nuclear family remains the 'traditional' model, changes in Western Europe and North America have seen the modern family adapt and change. The US sitcom *Modern Family* is an excellent representation of how families have changed. Only one family represents the nuclear family. The other two are same-sex and step-families. The traditional male role is fulfilled by Jay Pritchett. He loves sports and has a fractured relationship with his gay son, Mitchell. Jay is divorced and married to Gloria, a much younger Colombian wife. Gloria has a son from a previous relationship and a baby with Jay. Gloria's age also places her in the same age bracket as her step-children, Mitchell and Claire. Mitchell is in a same-sex relationship with Cameron and they have adopted a daughter, Lily, from Vietnam. Jay's daughter is married to Phil Dunphy and they represent the traditional nuclear family. They have three children: Haley, Alex and Luke. While certain characters conform to the obligatory comedy stereotypes, the nuances also challenge the view that certain identities are fixed and 'traditional'.

Through the institution of marriage, we can see how the state has exerted control over sexuality, intimacy and relationships. We can also see how the state has stepped back from regulating people's intimate lives. While a marriage of wife, husband and children has been the most common family structure in Western Europe and North America since the 17th century, it became increasingly linked to industrialisation. We often equate Victorian society with sexual reticence and conservatism. In 1866 case law in Britain defined marriage as between one man and one woman. Historically other religions and cultures have permitted polygamy, but nearly always in ways that placed the husband at the centre. Marriage was based on the gender-based social order. Men were the wage earners and operated in the public sphere, compared to women who inhabited the private space of the home. Women were tasked with looking after children. Sex was purely for procreation, rather than recreation. Despite the popularity of Romantics like Lord Byron, Samuel Taylor Coleridge and Percy Shelley, Victorians did not necessarily marry for love. Love was something that would grow within the marriage. Marriage was not about romance and passionate sex, but shared family values, religion and social class. These views continued until the 1970s and still permeate today.

As marriage has declined, cohabiting has increased. With a significant change in how people live their lives, there also comes a challenge to wider social perceptions. In *The Lonely Crowd* (1950) the US sociologist David Riesman divided society into two groups: inner directed and other directed. Inner directed people internalised their social values, while other directed individuals engaged with others relatively. This fits to the more performative approaches to identity of Erving Goffman and Judith Butler. For those inner directed individuals who see themselves and society as more fixed and 'natural', then changes to how people live their lives is a moral challenge. It is for this reason that the 1980s and 1990s witnessed a range of moral panics, principally around the family. The spread of HIV/AIDS was linked to declining morals. As we saw in Chapter 6, the US sociologist Charles Murray (1990) identified single mothers and children born out of wedlock as a leading indicator of crime and unemployment. We can see how this links to wider debates about the welfare state. As the neoliberal state has sought to reduce its expenditure on welfare, payments to single mums and their unemployed children became an easy target. Yet this was tied in with a broader moral concern about the changing role of the family and the decline in marriages.

What is interesting about relationships is that they are seen as the norm. Those who choose to not have a relationship are seen as the exception; there is something wrong with them. In *Going Solo: The Extraordinary Rise and Surprising Appeal of Living Alone* (2012), US sociologist Eric Klinenberg highlights how there are more people choosing to live as singles. For Klinenberg, this is predominately down to the economic prosperity of the post-war period that allows people to be able to afford to live on their own. But property prices have steadily increased, so this cannot be the only factor. He also suggests that there are four other factors:

- the rising status of women,
- communication technology,
- mass urbanisation, and
- people living longer.

Health and nutrition have improved which means that we have an ageing population. But if one person from the couple dies early, then the other partner is likely to live longer as a single. As we saw in the previous chapter, feminism and the empowerment of women has enabled many to distinguish themselves in their own right, independently of men. Traditionally, women were the property of the male, passed from father to husband. The right to vote and, more importantly, control over their own bodies, has permitted women to delay childbirth and marriage, or not to engage in either. Communication technology has also enabled more people to remain single. Television, as US political scientist Robert Putnam said in *Bowling Alone*, encourages the removal of people from public life (see Box 6.1). But the internet and social media enable us to communicate with people anywhere in the world at any time; the classic time-space compression of globalisation. Singletons who live in cities are also more likely to communicate face to face. As the city has become the focus of the new global economy, young educated people are working in urban areas that have a range of leisure activities that can mitigate the isolating experience of being single.

Once again there is the suggestion that we are becoming more individualistic. If more people are living alone, then doesn't this indicate that the individualism thesis is correct? This is why a sociological imagination is important. We should not simply look at the obvious to understand this; as sociologists we see the trend as a motive for us to investigate further and look beneath the surface. Klinenberg (2012: 18) highlights the opposite of individualism:

> It does not mean that those who live alone are condemned to feel lonely or be isolated. On the contrary, the evidence suggests that people who live alone compensate by becoming more socially active than those who live with others, and that cities with high numbers of singletons enjoy a thriving public culture.

While we may be exploring our own individual identity, it does not mean that we are isolating ourselves from wider public life. Those living in thriving cities have more opportunities to engage in public life, political groups, sport, leisure and socialising. Often, the parts of a city with the highest number of singletons are the most thriving places to go for a night out.

Box 6.1: Robert Putnam's *Bowling Alone*

Robert Putnam in *Bowling Alone* (2000) discussed growing individualism in the US. While the same number of people go bowling as they did 50 years ago, they go alone, rather than as part of a group. He equates this with a decline in 'social capital'. This is the network of relations we have with other people. Putnam suggested that during the 1950s and 1960s, there was a golden age of associationism where people joined local associations, religious groups, unions and workplace activities. Putnam highlights how our changing employment patterns and social lives have contributed to this situation. Because of the restructuring of the economy, many people have moved to new cities in order to find work which has separated them from their friends and family. Alternatively, they are commuting further in order to work which gives them less time to engage in charitable or civic activities. Individuals and families in the suburbs predominantly stay at home to watch television rather than engage in wider public life. All of these contribute, along with a wide range of social factors, such as class, gender, race and ethnicity, to a decline in public engagement and a sense of community.

Technology has changed how people meet, have sex and form relationships. Where some people 'drift' into relationships, others actively seek them online. Our working and social lives have become more fractured due to changing work patterns, especially in global cities. Social media, dating sites and apps, and the internet more widely, have dramatically opened up possibilities to meet new sexual and intimate partners. Websites like Ashley Madison even give opportunities to have affairs. Apps like Tinder and Grindr enable us to present an idealised or sexualised version of ourselves for others' consumption, a good example of Erving Goffman's 'presentation of self'. We carefully select images and text that will present a version of ourselves that we think will allow us to meet someone. Sex and relationships have become what Spanish sociologist Manuel Castells calls the 'network society'. Even those people who meet 'offline' in pubs, work or through friends, use social media to communicate to build and maintain their relationship. They stay in almost constant contact through Snapchat, WhatsApp or Facebook. Social media permits us to stay in almost constant virtual contact with our friends. Every aspect of our lives can be shared for friends to see and consume.

Sexualities

Chapters 3, 4 and 5 have shown us that race, class and gender are not fixed. Our identities are much more fluid and flexible depending on who is our audience. The previous chapter discussed this in relation to gender and the same argument applies to sexuality. As British sociologist Lynn Jamieson (1998: 128) states, 'sexuality is not predetermined but produced through specific practices'. Our individual sense of self and desires are shaped by society and enacted through practice. If sex is natural and about genital pleasure, then why are breasts considered sexual in some cultures? Why do we kiss or hold hands? If sex is naturally about reproduction, then why do we masturbate or use contraception? Why are others asexual? These are shaped by our own identities and desires in relation to wider society. After the Second World War, the nuclear family was premised on the heterosexual couple of a man and woman as husband and wife. British sociologist Ken Plummer notes in *Telling Sexual Stories* (1995: 123) that 'something dramatic happened to sexuality during the 1960s and 1970s'. Sex came to be viewed as beneficial and positive, it could be recreational, and it became more prevalent in popular culture. We can see this development by contrasting the sexual innuendo of British comedy in the 1960s, with its seemingly infinite euphemisms for sex and parts of the body, to the proliferation of pornography and sexualised images in the media. This period also resulted in a greater awareness of female sexuality. Feminist books like Nancy Friday's *My Secret Garden* (1973) and *The Female Eunuch* (1970) by Germaine Greer emphasised that women had sexual desires and fantasies too.

Sexual liberation during the 1960s also challenged the presumption of heterosexuality. Until then, homosexuality was seen as a deviant act that was outlawed. Anal sex with either gender was punishable by death until 1861. The Criminal Law Amendment Act 1885, along with raising the age of consent for sex with a woman from 12 to 16, also criminalised any kind of sexual acts between men. It was under this Act that Oscar Wilde was famously found guilty of gross indecency with Lord Alfred Douglas. Same-sex acts between women were notably excluded. The result was a society that was 'heteronormative' – the norm for society was heterosexuality, or what US poet Adrienne Rich (1980) calls 'compulsory heterosexuality'. The case of British computer science pioneer Alan Turing exemplifies the way that gay men were seen in the UK after the war. Turing was the leading intellect who helped break the Enigma Code that contributed to the defeat of the Nazis in the Second World War. After the war Turing returned to mathematics. One day, a friend of his gay lover burgled Turing's house. Turing reported the crime to the police and in the course of the proceedings acknowledged that he had a sexual relationship with the burglar's male friend. The police prosecuted Turing under the 1885 Act, where he was found guilty and sentenced to undergo hormonal treatment to reduce his libido, which rendered him impotent and prompted breast growth. He lost his security clearance at GCHQ (Government Communication Headquarters), but kept his academic job. Two years later he died by suicide. Turing's role in the war effort did not protect him from social views on his sexuality.

Homosexuality stopped being illegal after the Sexual Offences Act 1967, among the range of other legislation that removed the barriers to sexuality, race and gender. It was not until the 21st century that gays and lesbians have been accorded equality before the law. The age of consent for heterosexual and homosexual sex was equalised under the Sexual Offences (Amendment) Act 2000. Four years later legislation permitted lesbians and gays to have civil partnerships, while same-sex marriage was legalised in 2013. Until this point, people living in same-sex relationships were not afforded the legal rights of even heterosexual couples cohabiting. Same-sex couples were permitted to adopt from 2002 and lesbian couples who had children through in-vitro or assisted fertilisation were given equal parental rights. As we've seen elsewhere, equality legislation does not automatically mean equality in society. But it demonstrates a long battle by lesbian, gay, bisexual and transsexual (LGBT) activists since the 1960s.

Discussions of sexuality are intimately linked to poststructuralist discussions about identity. The work of people like Erving Goffman and Judith Butler highlight how we perform our identity based on the audience and social world around us. Sexuality is an excellent example of performativity. Because we still live in a broadly heteronormative world, homosexuals and bisexuals frequently have to 'come out'. The phrase is shortened from the idea that gay women and men had to live in the closet and hide their sexuality from the world. In this way they had to act straight in everyday life. It is for this reason that one of the ways of celebrating equality of sexuality is through Pride events. It reflects people identifying as LGBT being able to say that they are 'out and proud'. The use of the word 'pride' also reflects another emotion, that of shame. Hiding in the closest can be associated with shame, particularly in a heteronormative social world.

Sexuality can be seen as a continuum, with homosexuality and heterosexuality as being at different ends, with bisexuality in between. In *Making Sexual History* (2000) British sociologist Jeffrey Weeks observes how we are moving towards a more 'fluid' conception of sexuality that celebrates diversity. Anthony Giddens (1992) also suggests that as sex has become separated from reproduction, people can be more creative sexually leading to a 'plastic sexuality'. Heterosexuals were deemed to fall into preordained sexualities, while gay men and women had to reinvent themselves, but freed from some of the constraints of heteronormative lives. Rather than fall into traditional heteronormative roles, many people explore their feelings and sexualities, particularly as they mature from adolescence to adulthood. Some of these experiences are brief and experimental, others develop into something more meaningful. Some people may have same-sex sexual activities with one gender, but more durable intimate relationships with the other gender. For others, they may be more equal depending on the partner. In *Dual Attraction* (Weinberg et al, 1995), people who identify as bisexual are often initially confronted with feelings of confusion. This is followed by possibly thinking about being homosexual followed by acceptance of settling into an identity as bisexual. Again, this sexual fluidity causes anger and a lack of acceptance from those who see identities as absolutes. For these people, one is either male or female, straight or gay. As we have seen elsewhere, identity is more fluid, but still linked to pre-existing traditions, ideas and practices.

Most discussion of sexuality is centred on people actually having sex. For others, sex is not an important part of their identity. For some people, lack of sex is forced on them through the lack of available partners, for example. Others may have a lack of sexual attraction to any gender. For those who identify as asexual, our hypersexualised world is more alien. In *Understanding Asexuality* (2015), Canadian psychologist Anthony Bogaert argues that it is important for us to understand asexuality as it helps us understand our own sexualities. Just as learning about homosexuality forces us to confront assumptions about heterosexuality, understanding asexuality does the same for sexuality in general. As we will look at in the next section, we often link romance, sex, intimacy and love. Being asexual does not automatically mean that one cannot be in a romantic, loving and intimate relationship.

With the exploration of non-heterosexual sexualities, it should not be assumed that heterosexuality is fixed. Heterosexual sexuality is also something that needs to be learned and enacted in practice. The sexual revolution of the 1960s and feminism have helped to transform some aspects of women's sexualities. There are many myths around heterosexuality that are explicitly linked to gender. The romantic notion is that the male wins and sustains the love of a female. This is linked to notions of hegemonic masculinity and passive femininity. Women are seduced by men. Men are expected to be 'up for' sex all the time. Sex is something that men 'do' to women, which suggests that sex is not about reciprocal pleasure. British sociologist Stevi Jackson notes that 'we all learn to be sexual within society in which "real sex" is defined as a quintessentially heterosexual act, vaginal intercourse, and in which sexual activity is thought of in terms of an active subject and a passive object' (1996: 23). Sex is seen as about penetrative sex with the focus on male pleasure with the act concluding with the male orgasm. With the focus on male pleasure, heterosexual women continue to prioritise male pleasure over their own desires. Sexual desire has traditionally been seen as masculine and women encounter difficulty expressing this, even in long-term relationships. As we will see in the next section, women frequently have to undertake the 'emotion work' to manage their own emotions to maintain the relationship.

Despite greater gender equality and changes to heterosexual female sexuality, gendered assumptions remain. In *Modern Couples?* (2013), Dutch sociologist Jenny van Hooff highlights that, while there has been a transformation in heterosexuality since the 1960s, and women are not stigmatised about having sex before marriage or with multiple partners, there are still gendered double standards. Women can be socially branded for an excessive number of partners, where the same 'rules' don't apply to men. Even though there has been a loosening of sexual expectations, there is still a sexual double standard between men and women. This goes even further with revenge porn (see Box 6.2). Despite the sexual freedom for women, there is also an assumption that the ultimate goal is to find a long-term male partner. Any promiscuity and experimentation for heterosexual men and women are time-limited before 'settling down'. This links to another unwritten rule of heterosexuality: monogamy. Long-term monogamous commitment characterises the heterosexual relationship. Rather than being liberated to explore other intimate and sexual relationships, heterosexual couples, and women in particular, are expected to be monogamous. Monogamy is just assumed. This is not to say that these ideas and practices are wrong, but the sociological imagination enables us to question received wisdom and 'common sense'.

Box 6.2: 'Sexting', coercion and revenge porn

Changes in technology have also impacted intimacy. The proliferation of smartphones has created many opportunities to engage in different forms of sexual intimacy. This can range from 'sexting', where the participants exchange text messages of a sexual nature, to the exchange of naked or sexual photographs. In a trusting relationship, these exchanges can heighten sexual and physical intimacy and excitement. However, with greater access to technology that facilitates sexual imagery, there are also more opportunities for coercion, bullying and retribution, all of which can have significant impact on the victim's mental health and wellbeing. This can relate to sexual imagery being sent without consent to another person, as well as the unauthorised release of intimate data to others. Many young people, especially females, report feeling intimidated or coerced into sharing intimate images. These interactions can have a range of consequences which from increased popularity to gaining a new boyfriend or girlfriend through to shame or bullying. 'Revenge porn' is a specific phenomenon where intimate text or photographs taken within a trusting relationship are shared after that relationship has broken down.

Intimacy and love

Sociology helps us to unpick different aspects of social life, from society and identity to love and intimacy. As Lyn Jamieson states in *Intimacy* (1998: 106), 'sex, love and intimacy are analytically separate but in social practices they are often linked, as the phrase "making love" illustrates'. Romance tells us that we fall in love and that this is who we have sex with; we learn to make love. Over time we develop an intimacy with that person and sex and intimacy become linked. Despite attempts to suggest that humans are rational beings, we are emotional. As German sociologist Georg Simmel (1950) noted about sociability, we enjoy the pleasure of people for its own sake. Many people seek friendships, sexual companions and life partners because of the emotions generated within the relationship. French sociologist Emile Durkheim observed how groups created a 'collective effervescence' that generated a sense of belonging to the group. This emotion helps produce solidarity between individuals and helps explain the feelings of love, passion and joy that exist within the smallest group of two people in a couple.

By analysing everyday life, we can see how society has changed and stayed the same. Despite changes to legislation and culture, certain inequalities persist. While old forms of solidarity are loosening and breaking, people are making new groups around consumption and identity. We can see this pattern replicated with marriage, relationships and love. As we've seen above, the institution of marriage has become weakened and the divorce rate has risen sharply over the past four decades. Yet people still spend thousands of pounds on their weddings, and gay marriage shows that the symbol of marriage is still important in the 21st century, including for many non-Christian cultures. Sex has become liberated from marriage and having one sexual partner for life is no longer expected. Yet long-term monogamous relationships are still desired. While it was expected that love and intimacy would result from marriage, these characteristics of relationships have changed as our relationships have changed.

Anthony Giddens (1990, 1991, 1992) and Ulrich Beck, the individualists of 'reflexive modernity', think that love and intimacy have been freed from previous meanings and given significance by the individuals in the relationship. German sociologists Beck and Beck-Gernsheim (1995; 2002) suggest that in our intimate lives, love is given its own meaning and it has become central. They argue 'for individuals who have to invent or find their own social setting, love becomes the central pivot giving meaning to their lives' (Beck and Beck-Gernsheim, 1995: 170). They do this directed 'by the lyrics of pop songs, advertisements, pornographic scripts, light fiction' (Beck and Beck-Gernsheim, 1995: 5). The continued success of romantic novels and films like *Jane Eyre*, or more recently *Fifty Shades of Grey*, potentially confirm this. But the sociological imagination is about linking the personal to the public and finding people's own meanings for their lives. With something like love and intimacy, this is highly personal. At the same time, it is still affected by consumer culture around us.

Anthony Giddens suggests in *The Transformation of Intimacy* (1992) that, because sex has become decoupled (pun intended) from marriage and reproduction, we now have a new kind of intense intimate relationship. Giddens (1992: 58) calls this 'the pure relationship' that

> refers to a situation where a social relation is entered into for its own sake, for what can be derived by each person from a sustained association with another; and which is continued only in so far as it is thought by both parties to deliver enough satisfaction for each individual to stay within it.

This intense emotional relationship is built through 'disclosing intimacy' and reflexively considering the other person's emotions and needs. As each have to maintain the relationship, Giddens suggests that there is a move to greater gender equality. Despite this theoretical assertion, gender differences persist, as we've seen this throughout this book. Furthermore, Lynn Jamieson (1998) argues against Giddens' (and others) individualisation argument by highlighting that in practice humans have a range of different intimate relationships with lovers, friends and family. There is not simply a mutually disclosing intimacy with lovers and an awareness of others. We do not have one partner with whom we share everything. Some things we share with family members, other secrets with best friends with different intimate experiences with a sexual partner. Despite some dramatic changes to relationships and intimacy, many previous emotions, traditions and inequalities endure.

Love still has meaning for individuals. It becomes a 'legitimating ideology' in the words of Lee Comer (1974). It legitimates marriage and commitment. But this does not mean that love is easy to talk about, or even to define. British sociologist Julia Carter (2013: 733) shows that many people 'drift' into relationships, 'rather than romantic tales of falling "head over heels"'. Many people don't talk of love until prompted. Love grows from within those relationships. Individual biography is also important. Where there is a history of relationship breakup, there is more reticence to talk of 'love'. This links to the romantic ideal that true love is once in a lifetime. In *The Commercialisation of Intimate Life* (2003) US sociologist Arlie Hochschild calls this the 'modern paradox of love'. As love has become commercialised, we see stories of whirlwind romances, love at first sight, and people being swept off their feet. However, we know that there are increasing divorce rates and we have previous relationships to tell us that love is far from eternal. In reality love is more pragmatic with relationships often forming between friends. This links to Anthony Giddens' (1992: 61) idea of 'confluent love' where there is an 'opening oneself out to the other'. Love is changing and adapts over time. We rationalise the love of past relationships to lower the emotion as though it is not possible to love more than one person in a lifetime. Despite Giddens and Beck and Beck-Gernsheim's assertions, love still draws on its earlier understandings.

Sex and sexuality have driven many of the social changes since the 1960s. Ken Plummer writes in *Telling Sexual Stories* (1995) that different ways of discussing intimacy have driven an 'intimate citizenship' that offers new ways of mobilising and forming new social groups. In *Invented Moralities* (1995) Jeffrey Weeks suggests that this 'radical humanism' allows us to accept and respect difference as a result of this changing sexual situation. Many of the liberalisation of laws governing people's personal lives have come through feminist and LGBT activists campaigning for the right to control their own bodies and who they have sex with. US sociologist Judith Stacey argues *In The Name of the Family* (1996) that lesbian and gay families denote a new ideal of marriage and contemporary relationships because they are freed of traditional gendered assumptions of the female and male role. While this has opened up the possibility of new ways of engaging in relationships, such as having civil partnerships, other forms of intimate relationship continue, including marriage.

Intimacy is not simply related to physical intimacy. We have a variety of emotional, physical and spiritual needs and who we share these details with is an important part of intimacy. Self disclosure of information links back to Erving Goffman's 'presentation of self'. Detailing our personal secrets determines how we feel about our friends and partners. Best friends will often know more information than work colleagues or acquaintances. In *The Managed Heart* (1983) Arlie Hochschild highlighted how we have to undertake 'emotional labour' to manage our emotions in the workplace, particularly in the service sector. This can be extended to the private space of the home as couples have to do 'emotion work' to adapt to the other. British sociologists Jean Dunscombe and Dennis Marsden (1993) focus on the importance of emotional intimacy in heterosexual relationships. They paint an essentialised picture of men and women having different physical and emotional needs. In an overly binary picture, they highlight how men have difficulty expressing their emotions and women grow increasingly frustrated with the lack of emotional intimacy. While it is problematic to reduce emotional engagement into binary genders, it does reiterate the performance of gender, as we saw in Chapter 5. Socially, men and women are expected to engage with emotion and emotional intimacy in different ways. The performance of hegemonic masculinity requires men to supress emotion, particularly emotions that could be considered as vulnerabilities, like fear, anxiety or even love. It is for this reason that there are statements like 'boys don't cry'. As we showed in Chapter 5, emotion is often considered feminine and, through sociable friendship groups, many women become more skilled at articulating their feelings than men. More often, this results in heterosexual women doing the 'emotional labour' to adapt to their male partners.

Awareness of this male emotional deficit became prominent in the 1990s with the rise of the 'new man'. This challenged hegemonic views of masculinity that had become dominant. This coincided with a growing literature on masculinity, like Australian sociologist Raewyn Connell's 'hegemonic masculinity' (1987, 1995). At the same time there was a growing feminisation of the workplace that has come about through growing equality legislation and changes to global demands in the economy. As much of the informational economy is based on the creative industries and the service sector, managing emotions is important. As Arlie Hochschild (1983) shows, 'emotional labour' is very important in the service industries. Having better emotional intelligence in the workplace impacts on access to the workplace and can exclude certain forms of masculinity. The 'new man' was expected to manage their emotion in the workplace, as well as taking a more central role in fatherhood, and be more equitable over domestic duties. This also contributed to the backlash from the 'new lad' that we covered in Chapter 5.

Sexuality, love, intimacy and relationships are some of the many ways that we can see how social life has changed, particularly since the 1960s. The hard fought battles by gay rights activists and feminists have brought about a growing awareness and acceptance of sexualities other than male heterosexuality. There has been a growing equality within heterosexual relationships as female sexuality has become less taboo. Successful campaigns have also equalised many rights for lesbian and gays to marry and adopt children, as well as opening up new possibilities and acceptance of other forms of sexuality. Despite these changes, being heterosexual, married and having children is still seen as the norm in some sections of society. As such, many pre-existing inequalities continue. Heterosexual relationships are still unequal, with women expected to manage their emotions and desires. Sex remains male-oriented and focused on penetrative intercourse and male orgasm. Long-term monogamous relationships remain the goal for many men and women.

KEY POINTS SUMMARY

- The nuclear family is a social construct that originated after the Second World War. Historically, families were extended and diverse with child-rearing responsibilities spread across a wide variety of members of the community.
- Intimacy, sex and love are all distinct, but often get entwined into how we see relationships.
- Sexuality is a continuum, rather than binary, between heterosexuality and homosexuality. This also includes asexuality.

- Despite growing equality for women in society, inequalities and abuse continue within relationships, dating and everyday life through dating apps, revenge porn and #MeToo.

KEY READING GUIDE

- *Bowling Alone* (2000) became an influential text on the decline of communities. Robert Putnam argued that more people were withdrawing from everyday life due to television, companies moving cities and greater commuting times. All of these meant that people didn't invest in their communities. *Bowling Alone* promotes a particular type of US community and invariably equates community engagement with positive social outcomes. Community engagement can still bring about inequalities, however. The Ku Klux Klan were invested in their local white community, to the exclusion of non-whites.

- In *Intimacy: Personal Relationships in Modern Societies* (1998), Jamieson argues against the individualisation of society by highlighting the variety of ways that humans relate with each other. Intimacy is not just about disclosure of secrets, but a variety of activities including spending time with people, giving gifts, feeling attachment, caring for others and more. There are many different ways of being intimate in a wide variety of relationships. Some of these may be found in the same person, but it is not always easy to find love, sex, intimacy and friendship in one person.

- In *Telling Sexual Stories* (1995), Ken Plummer highlights the intimate role that sex plays in everyday life. While we are inundated with images of sex, there are still significant aspects of our sexual histories and sexualities that are intimate and secret. Through inquiring into these intimate stories, Plummer highlights how they are part of everyday life, and how they help the narrator of these stories to make sense of the episode, activity and themselves.

- 'Sex sells' as the old adage goes. In *The Commercialisation of Intimate Life* (2003), Arlie Hochschild shows that it is not just sex that has been commodified and sold back to us, but every aspect of our family life. From nurseries, to schools, to university, our education is being made part of a market, as are care for older relatives and our health and wellbeing, from gyms to medicine. The same is true for celebrations with professional caterers for weddings, birthday parties and dinner parties all becoming private businesses, encroaching into the private life of the family.

7

Globalisation and post-industrialisation

The biggest political and social crisis in recent British memory has been the decision to leave the European Union (EU). On Thursday 23 June 2016, of those that voted in the referendum, 52 per cent voted for the UK to leave the EU. The following day, Prime Minister David Cameron stood on the doorstep of 10 Downing Street and announced that he would take responsibility and resign. While noble, this decision ignited chaos. The Conservative Party turned inwards and the leadership battle that had been latent for months came to the fore. Theresa May emerged as prime minister and was immediately confronted with trying to unite her party and the country. The Official Opposition, the Labour Party, was also beset with internal divisions with centrist and pro-European MPs battling with their new left-wing and suspiciously anti-EU leader, Jeremy Corbyn. These party-political battles have continued through to the ascension of Boris Johnson to the prime ministerial role, and are likely to continue beyond, whatever trajectory Brexit takes.

This chapter looks at the role of political economy: the relationship between the state and the economy. Through an overview of the foundations of political economy through to its impact on globalisation, we will see how the UK has shifted from an industrial to a post-industrial society and how this has affected the country, before assessing how this could account for the divisions exposed during and since the referendum on EU membership. The referendum reignited conversations about the impact of globalisation.

Under-investment, poverty and migration were all factors for many people voting to leave. The result highlighted a highly polarised society. Most importantly, it clearly showed the divisions that had occurred since the UK engaged on a process of de-industrialisation and neoliberal globalisation. Manchester, London and key cities such as Brighton and Hove, Bristol, Oxford and Cambridge voted to remain within the EU. The shires, towns and cities greatly affected by de-industrialisation voted to leave the EU. The referendum became a barometer against globalisation. Across the country, graduates were more likely to vote to stay in the EU compared to those without a university-level education, highlighting how the global economy was permitting access to those with certain skills, yet excluding others. Further demographic cleavages were revealed. The majority of younger people voted to remain, while older voters remembering a time before these changes voted to leave. And among all this, Scotland voted overwhelmingly to stay in the EU and now agitated to remain, angry at another English decision overriding its interests. Overall, the EU referendum provided a clear snapshot of the importance of sociology. It was not merely a simple question of remaining a member, but the consolidation of a wide range of social, economic and political factors that had been growing for over 30 years.

This polarisation has been exacerbated with austerity. In *Austerity Bites* (2014), journalist Mary O'Hara travelled the country to talk to those at the cutting edge of government cuts. As part of their political project to cut the deficit after the financial crash, the coalition (2010–15) and Conservative (2015–) governments consistently cut welfare spending to the most vulnerable in society. O'Hara identified four reasons for austerity measures adversely affecting the poor: lack of employment; casualisation of the jobs market; low pay and stagnating wages; increased sanctions for non-compliance to new government policies. The neoliberal agenda (see Box 7.2) behind austerity was also reflected in the savage cuts to local government and jobs in the public sector. O'Hara highlighted how London and the South East of England were the least dependent on public sector employment, and the public sector cuts disproportionately hit those areas that had the fewest private sector jobs. And these were the areas that had been already negatively affected by de-industrialisation.

Political economy

Economic activity is – to some extent – regulated by the state. It is negotiated, worked for, related to different sets of values, and changing all the time. In short: all economic relations are political. Classical theories of economics, in particular the work of Scottish economist Adam Smith, pointed to a liberal market-led approach with minimal government interference. This approach is called *laissez-faire* and comes from the French to 'let do' and refers to an economic approach with minimal regulation. In *The Wealth of Nations* (1776) Smith referred to the 'invisible hand' of the market that guided the actions of individuals. In reality there is not an 'invisible hand' controlling the markets. If you had an invisible hand, would you use it to control the economy? People run the economy and markets; they are social. Yet for Smith, social action is reducible to monetary action. The free market, while appearing chaotic and unrestrained, will produce what is needed. Significantly, Smith highlighted the importance of 'division of labour'. He analysed production in a pin factory and concluded that when different parts of the manufacturing process were broken down into their constituent parts, then the factory would produce significantly more pins than if one individual made one pin at a time.

In contrast to Adam Smith and other classical economists, Karl Marx identified a number of other significant aspects within the capitalist process. Marx is more famous for his political activism and ideas supporting Communism. These were based on his economic analyses, yet Marx was also a philosopher, social theorist, historian and journalist (see Box 7.1). Significantly for sociology, he synthesised these diverse disciplines and identified the social relations within capitalism. More importantly, he identified the role of power within the division of labour identified by Adam Smith. For Marx, there is a power dynamic between the capitalists (the bourgeoisie) who own the businesses and the proletariat, the workers whose labour is exploited. The owners of the means of production have power to buy the labour of the working classes at less than market price. The difference is the profit extracted by the capitalists. As mentioned in Chapter 4, for Marx the struggle between the working classes and the owners of the means of production was what defined society. In *The Communist Manifesto* (written with his friend Friedrich Engels in 1848), Marx suggests that, 'The history of all hitherto existing society is the history of class struggles.' This conflict produced the changes and challenges that shaped social action.

In contrast to Smith and Marx, Max Weber saw religion as a key contributor to the emergence of capitalism. In *The Protestant Ethic and the Spirit of Capitalism* (1905), Weber argued that Protestants, particularly Calvinists, believed in predestination, which meant that they had already been destined to go to heaven. In order to prove this, they had to work hard to show their piety and devotion to God. This belief aligned itself with the pursuit of profit and material wealth. Early Protestants eschewed wealth, but the development of the US helped to break down social barriers to wealth generation. In Europe many trades were still controlled by guilds, which led to social shame if a guild member was earning more than the others, as it would have been at their acquaintances' expense. Weber observed that in the US businessmen (and they were all men) congregated around their church, rather than their profession. Consequently, they were no longer bound by the social norms of the profession, but by their religion. As wealth was seen as the quantifiable reward for hard work and, by extension, their devotion to God, then they were encouraged to create wealth. Once capitalism had become entrenched as the acceptable way of organising the market, it continued (and continues) to go through a process of 'rationalisation'. For Weber, capitalism, and society in general, is continually pushed to be more 'rational' to remove the emotion, traditions and inefficiencies in society in order to make it more efficient and bureaucratic. In this way, religion has been discarded from capitalism.

While both Smith and Marx (and others) have reduced social activity to economic activity, it is possible to see how society is shaped through changes to political economy. Political decisions help

Box 7.1: Marxism

Marxism is a complex term that can mean a variety of things to different audiences. Part of the reason for this is due to the extensive writings of Karl Marx and the numerous interpretations and re-interpretations of his work. Born in Germany, before moving in exile to Paris, Brussels and then London, Marx was a political agitator, journalist and scholar. He wrote on philosophy, history, economics and politics, and is regarded as one of the pioneers of sociology principally due to his recognition of the social aspects of capitalism. This contrasted sharply with analyses at the time that saw each individual as a standalone island. Central to Marx's analysis is the social relationship between workers and the owners of the means of production. For Marx, all of society was structured by this relationship and the resultant class struggle as the means of production were owned by the bourgeoisie and workers toiled for them for wages which did not reflect the full value of what they produced. This resulted in the workers being alienated from their labour; they could not actualise their own self-identity because of this exploitation. Elsewhere in this book, and later in this chapter, we see many cases of individuals being able to explore their own identities. Despite this, exploitation and structural inequalities continue, specifically around race, gender and class.

determine what role the market plays in social life. Political economy has oscillated between the *laissez-faire* approach advocated by Adam Smith to a more state-oriented approach (and back again). From the industrial revolution until the Depression of the 1930s, the British government maintained a laissez-faire approach. From the end of the Second World War until the 1970s, the state was seen an as important control on what British sociologist John Maynard Keynes called the 'animal spirits' of the market, as markets did not work for the benefit of society but for the people running them. It was felt that the role of government was to provide employment for the population and economic security. Keynes proposed an interventionist policy that meant that the government would use fiscal and monetary measures to mitigate the worst effects of recessions, depressions and booms. By the 1970s, the work of Adam Smith was revived by neoliberal economists like the US economist Milton Friedman who called for the state to step away from the market. It is called neoliberal ('neo' means 'new') because it is a new version of the liberal economics of Adam Smith. The result has been a transformation of global interconnectivity, as well as a change in how the economy is organised and what jobs are available.

Globalisation

Conversations about globalisation re-emerged on the social and political landscape during the election of Donald Trump and the Brexit referendum. Globalisation is a contested term. It is important to a narrative about the EU because many of the issues raised by voters throughout the referendum campaign (and after it) were actually related to globalisation. Issues like jobs, investment, skills, migration and 'taking back control' are all outcomes of a changing global economy and related cultural changes.

There are a number of themes within the plentiful definitions of globalisation. This section focuses on the changing role of political economy and capitalism. Other chapters highlight cultural changes, particularly around identity, consumption and lifestyles. Associated technological advances have helped the impact of globalisation, leading to a compression of time and space that makes the world feel more interconnected. Yet at the same time, it can lead to a feeling of helplessness. As the British sociologist Anthony Giddens states in *The Consequences of Modernity* (1990: 64), 'Globalization can thus be defined as the intensification of worldwide social relations which link distinct localities in such a way that local happenings are shaped by events occurring many miles away and vice versa.' Many of the changes that have taken place in the UK have been as the result of changing political and economic processes around the globe. While the EU was seen as responsible by those seeking to leave, it is merely one part of a much wider, globalised world. This demonstrates how we are becoming more aware of the world around us.

The Extinction Rebellion movement is indicative of this. A non-violent socio-political movement that started in mid-2018 in the UK spread across the world in 2019 with protestors drawing acute and dramatic attention to the threat of climate change and loss of biodiversity by organising petitions, rallies, blockades and sit-ins. Old techniques and ideologies of dissent with new means of technology and organisation have combined to provide sustained, coordinated protest to imminent threats to humanity.

As US sociologist Roland Robertson argues in *Globalization* (1992: 8), 'Globalization as a concept refers to both the compression of the world and the intensification of consciousness of the world as a whole.' The global consciousness permits us to think of events with global significance, such as environmentalism, while also providing a sociological imagination for events that affect us as individuals.

Yet globalisation is not a 'thing' that exists outside us, it is a set of processes that have been enacted by various individuals making

Figure 7.1: Extinction Rebellion protestors in central London, November 2018

Source: © Copyright David Holt, London November 23 2018 (19) Extinction Rebellion Protest Tower Hill, www.flickr.com/photos/zongo/31078299267/

political, economic and cultural decisions. It is also something that we do in our consumer and political choices. In *Global Transformations* (2000: 16), British political scientist David Held highlights how

> Globalization may be thought of as a process (or set of processes) which embodies a transformation in the spatial organization of social relations and transactions – assessed in terms of their extensity, intensity, velocity and impact – generating transcontinental or interregional flows and networks of activity, interaction and the exercise of power.

Therefore, globalisation is not just something that happened, but something that is in the process of happening. In this way we can see the world as an interconnected network of individuals, businesses and institutions.

Globalisation is not new. Extensive trade routes have existed since early civilisation. The most famous is the Silk Route that stretched from China in the east to Europe in the west. The roots of modern global capitalism can be traced to late Medieval Europe. European trade and capitalism originated around the Mediterranean as ancient trading networks were strengthened. Mediterranean and central European areas were at the core of European trade – especially around Flanders and Northern Italy. The strength of the guilds in Italy ensured that competition was minimised and strict regulations enforced. The contrast with England was sharp – if industrialists faced restrictive trade patterns, then they simply transferred their operations to other areas of the country. The British historian Niall Ferguson argued in *Empire* (2003) argued that this liberal, less centralised approach encouraged greater investment and creativity, particularly in the Netherlands and Britain (while glossing over many of the negative aspects of Empire).

Even though the British approach was founded on the notion of private companies and trade, it was supported by military power and racialised philosophies. Although private companies, like the South Sea Company and the East India Trading Company, operated monopolies in those areas, slavery maintained the British colonies in the West Indies, while Africa and India were kept in line by force. The East India Trading Company established a trading monopoly with India and capitalised on the growth of demand for Indian commodities during the industrial revolution. Effectively, the Company ruled India with military support from the British state. Any form of resistance from local populations was brutally crushed. In *Inglorious Empire*, Shashi Tharoor (2017), the Indian politician, highlighted the many ways that the British maintained their economic dominance. For example, the British didn't just break the looms of Indian textile workers so that British textiles would be competitive, they broke their fingers so they couldn't continue to work. As British sociologist Gurminder Bhambra argues in *Connected Sociologies* (2014), the global capitalist system was built on a system of thought infused with racialised colonial ideas. Most of the thinkers mentioned in this book would have developed their thinking within this environment and most take a Eurocentric (and masculine) focus to their analysis.

The British government supported this private mercantile trade in the empire through military support and deregulation. Free trade came into Britain with the repeal of the Corn Laws in 1846, which were effectively import tariffs to protect British grain prices from cheap imports. They were implemented in 1815, but with peace after Waterloo, foreign prices dropped and this ensured that grain prices were kept artificially high; the repeal of the Corn Laws meant the price of bread fell (and suppliers were hard hit). Liberal mercantile trade continued until the First World War, which then developed into a period of instability. British trading hegemony in the 19th century led to the pound being the *de facto* global currency. The British linked the value of the pound to the price of gold (the 'gold standard') in the late 19th century. The gold standard is important as it reflects how the global economy became linked together, but also how nation states sought to control their economies. The gold standard was removed after the First World War, as nation states wanted to try and control their own economies to rebuild after the war. However, this move was disastrous and led to hyperinflation, the Great Depression and ultimately the Second World War. The gold standard was re-adopted after the Second World War as nation states sought to bring some stability back. This coincided with a change to the way nations organised their economies, which we will see in the subsequent section on post-industrialisation. When US President Richard Nixon removed the US dollar from the gold standard in 1971, it precipitated the current economic climate and coincided with the dramatic awareness of globalisation.

Analysis of the Great Depression contributed to two economic approaches that have held dominance at two different times over the past 50 years. Immediately after the Second World War, Keynesian economics held sway and this led to a period of national control over state economies. After economic problems in the 1970s, neoliberal economics came to dominance, particularly under Ronald Reagan and Margaret Thatcher in the US and UK respectively. This approach removed the state from the economy and opened up national economies to a more globalised, interconnected approach. Neoliberalism, as advocated by US economist Milton Friedman and others, seeks to remove government interference in the economy (see Box 7.2). In *A Monetary History of the United States* (1963), Friedman argued that the Depression was caused by a lack of money in circulation. The financial crisis started as an ordinary recession but mistakes by the Federal Reserve restricted the money supply, which led to depression. For example, the Federal Reserve allowed large public banks like the New York Bank of the United States to collapse, which led to widespread panic and runs on local banks. This restricted the banks' ability to lend, so businesses were not able to obtain loans. The legacy of this was seen in UK Prime Minister Gordon Brown's policy of 'quantitative easing' during the financial crisis of 2007–08.

The prevailing economic view after the Second World War was based on the theories of British economist John Maynard Keynes. He argued that the Depression was caused by underconsumption and overinvestment. Keynes observed the paradox of thrift. As individuals feel concerned about their welfare, they reduce their expenditure. This in turn reduces the income of business. As their income falls, businesses rationalise their workforce, who in turn, reduce their expenditure. The result of everyone spending less is a contradiction of the economy. Keynes' argument was that a safety net should be installed that ensures that consumption is maintained. These views were given political traction in the UK after the war with the creation of the welfare state reinforced by a regulated national economy.

After the Second World War national economies across Western Europe and North America were underpinned by international agreement. Throughout this period, we saw the formation of international organisations between national governments. The origins of the EU can be traced to this trend. Elsewhere there was the military alliance of the North Atlantic Treaty Organisation (NATO) founded in 1949, the United Nations and the International Monetary Fund (IMF) both established in 1945, and the Commonwealth (1949). International trade was regulated through the General Agreement on Tariffs and Trade (GATT), formed in 1947 (and which became the World Trade Organisation in 1995). Other international organisations existed earlier, like the International Telecommunication Union, which administered radio frequencies (1865) before becoming an agency within the UN. Police cooperation has existed since the creation of Interpol in 1923.

Economic reconstruction in Western Europe came from economic support from the US in the shape of the Marshall Plan. This provided credit and trade for European and US businesses to help rebuild the continent. It also helped to incorporate Korea and Japan into the US trading system. The global south in Africa, Asia and Latin America was notable by its absence. The financial arrangement was established at the United Nations Monetary and Financial Conference held at Bretton Woods in 1944, which laid the foundations for extensive global economic integration. Bretton Woods implemented a Keynesian system of controlled or organised capitalism across the West. Governmental involvement in the economy would help to prevent under consumption and ensure that there was full employment. This was organised on Fordist principles, which will be covered in the next section. Inflation was controlled through increasing interests rates to prevent excessive consumption. Bretton

Woods also reinstated the gold standard to ensure a controlled exchange rate. The conference set up the IMF to provide short-term loans to overcome short-term economic instability and ensure that the international monetary system ran smoothly. The IMF was underpinned by the US dollar, even after the inflation/stagflation of the 1970s. Thus, the US dollar was effectively instigated as a common global currency. Alongside the IMF, the World Bank was set up to help provide funds for European reconstruction and later provided funds for industrial development in developing nations. All of this was underpinned by US military support, with US bases around the world and reinforced through NATO.

The Second World War also had two other dramatic impacts that affected the debate around the EU referendum in 2016. First, the post-war period saw anti-colonial and independence movements across the colonies of European empires. This resulted in most former colonies gaining independence between the 1940s and 1970s. Many of these colonies also saw widespread emigration to their former imperial rulers as the European nations needed human resources to help rebuild (as outlined in Chapter 3). Second, decolonisation affected the power and economies of the European nations. Europe had been at the forefront of the world economy at the start of the 20th century through its countries' empires. After the Second World War, European nations lost their empires and were challenged by US and Japan as industrial economies. This led to increased cooperation between European nations. The European Coal and Steel Community was established in 1952 to create a common market for coal and steel, the two commodities that underpinned the post-war industrial reconstruction of Europe. It was signed by Germany, France, Italy and the Benelux countries of Belgium, Netherlands and Luxemburg. Six years later these countries formed the European Economic Community (EEC) under the Treaty of Rome. These six countries were joined by Denmark, the UK, Ireland, Greece, Portugal and Spain over the following 30 years. These organisations formed the basis of the EU, which was formalised in the Maastricht Treaty of 1992 and which became the focus of the 2016 referendum in the UK.

Greater integration of the EEC occurred during the 1970s at a time when the Bretton Woods system began to collapse. The US dollar was the underpinning currency of the gold standard that supported the Bretton Woods agreement. Inflation in the US began increasing, partly due to the dollar being the global currency and partly because of US military spending on the Vietnam War. In response US President Richard Nixon decoupled the dollar from the gold standard and stopped fixed exchange rates (the 'Nixon shock'), which effectively implemented a neoliberal economy. The Yom Kippur War between Israel and a coalition of Arab states, including Syria and Egypt, exacerbated global economic problems in 1973. At the end of the year, the Organisation of Arab Petroleum Exporting Countries (OAPEC) declared an embargo on export of oil and restricted supply to Western economies. The stock markets crashed and Nixon began a process of US involvement in the Middle East to maintain peace. This period led to a period of 'stagflation' across Europe and North America, which involved high inflation and low growth; ultimately national economies could not grow themselves out of recession.

Across Europe, the 1970s saw the exhaustion of Fordist methods of production (which are covered in the next section and in Box 7.3), social upheaval through social and union agitation and widespread recession. These problems were exacerbated in the UK in 1976 when the Labour government under Jim Callaghan had to request a loan from the IMF to stabilise the pound. IMF and World Bank loans always come with stipulations to cut government expenditure, or austerity, and the social problems in the UK were made worse. The Winter of Discontent between 1978 and 1979 was caused by continued pay caps on public sector staff to control inflation. This led to widespread strikes during one of the coldest winters for two decades. The Conservative government under Margaret Thatcher won the subsequent general election in May 1979. A new economic orthodoxy was about to begin.

The Keynesian system had collapsed. Richard Nixon's decision to uncouple the dollar from the gold standard enabled financial speculators to invest in currency markets. The election of Margaret

Thatcher in the UK in 1979 and Ronald Reagan in the US in 1980 took this form of economic deregulation further. They provided political support for businesses agitating for access to global markets. The US economist Milton Friedman (1962, 1963) advocated a monetarist economic policy: the focus of governments should be to control the supply of money. This was a marked shift from the Keynesian approach that sought to control demand through policies affecting production and consumption. The growth of monetarism in the 1980s removed much of the political involvement in national economies, particularly in the US and UK. Reagan believed big government was the problem for stagflation and set about liberalising trade. The US was the prime instigator in liberalising trade during the Uruguay round of GATT negotiations from 1986. This approach was also reinforced through the Washington Consensus. Through the IMF and World Bank, the US forced neoliberal policies on nations across the world. Any national government taking out a loan from the IMF or World Bank was expected to implement policies that would limit governmental involvement in the economy, including the liberalisation of trade, privatisation of state enterprises, deregulation of financial markets and the reduction of state subsidies for businesses.

As Margaret Thatcher was a strong advocate of these deregulatory policies, they were being implemented in the UK anyway. State businesses were privatised, from coal and steel to British Telecom and energy companies. During the same year as the Uruguay round of GATT negotiations, the US and UK launched the Big Bang, which deregulated the financial industries and opened up financial trading across the globe. The result was that the British economy became more focused on financial trading in the City of London and less focused on industry, as we will see shortly. The impact of this can be traced to the financial crisis of 2007–08. It can also be witnessed in another news story of 2016 dubbed 'the Panama Papers'. Millions of leaked financial and legal documents showed how wealthy individuals were moving their money around the world in order to avoid paying tax. This had become the central narrative of neoliberalism. The global elite did not want to pay tax for national welfare states. With reduced tax, the institutions of state had to be privatised, reduced or closed.

Box 7.2: Neoliberalism and modern society

Neoliberalism is a broad concept that refers to a form of free market capitalism and economic liberalism. In its broadest sense, neoliberalism also refers to elements of individual choice, individualisation and individual responsibility, effectively removing any arguments of structural factors affecting people. Neoliberal capitalism is specifically a set of policies such as privatisation, deregulation and austerity which advocate a reduction in government spending and an increase in the activities and scope of the private sector. Neoliberalism is distinct from Keynesianism. The latter advocated for state involvement in the market to alleviate the extremes of the market, including recessions, inequalities and scarcity. In contrast, neoliberalism is about rolling back the state from economic matters and encouraging the 'free market'. In *The Road to Serfdom* (1944), economist and philosopher Friedrich Hayek argued that dictatorship and reduced democracy came from government control of the economy as they had to coerce consumers. In contrast, free market activities adjust without coercion from authority. This assumes all transactions are undertaken between people of equal power. Sociology highlights the power imbalances in society that can entrench inequalities. US economist Milton Friedman also paired neoliberalism with democracy in *Capitalism and Freedom* (1962). He assumed racism would impede capital accumulation as capitalists would employ the best people to help them make a profit. Not only does this ignore the history of slavery where black Africans were enslaved to help plantation owners profit, but it also ignores the inequalities that emerge from restricted access to opportunities and discrimination in society. Despite the focus on individual freedom, neoliberal policies have sought to deregulate collective action, especially trade unions. Breaking up collective solidarity creates a group of individuals who are all competing against each other, rather than a collective working together. In relation to significant social issues such as climate change, government and collective interventions are required but face opposition from those who argue that regulation would impede business.

With these neoliberal policies, the state was rolled back from the economy. Where international agreements after the war were about protecting national economies, since the 1980s, they have focused on protecting transnational corporations. As US political economist Robert Gilpin (2001: 75) suggests, 'Freeing financial markets also facilitated reorganization and transformation of international business. The unification of national financial markets encouraged the creation of a single, globally integrated market for corporation ownership and corporate takeover activities.' Corporations no longer focused on national markets. They sought to expand their business across the globe. Since the 1980s, transnational brands like Coca-Cola, McDonalds, Nike, Sony and Apple have become global symbols of consumption and in many cases have higher turnovers than many national economies. Liberalising trade not only enabled these corporations to sell their products globally but also permitted them to move their production to locations with the cheapest labour or best skills. In some cases, this was facilitated by changes to national policy elsewhere. In China, Deng Xiaoping created Special Enterprise Zones in cities like Shenzhen in 1980. This opened up these zones to foreign investment and saw Western businesses move their production, often meaning that they closed their factories in the US or Western Europe.

With the growth of US power, and the emergence of new economic powers like China, European influence was weakening. What had been the central economic region for centuries was being eclipsed in the new global economy. A new political project emerged to increase influence – economic, foreign policy and social integration. The Maastricht Treaty of 1992 implemented European Monetary Union, which eventually led to the Euro currency. Maastricht effectively imposed a set of economic criteria over member states, which included minimising government debt, annual deficits and linked exchange rates. It also underpinned the principles of the free movement of goods, services and people across the EU. Social provisions were also included, but the UK opted out of these. Alongside this, the US has entered into regional agreements with the North American Free Trade Association (NAFTA) with Canada and Mexico (1994).

Overall, the post-war period has covered two forms of globalisation. The first was reasserting the primacy of national governments and national economies. International agreements were ratified by nation states to cooperate on economic and military matters. The EEC was part of this general trend that included the UN, NATO, and the IMF. All of these underpinned national control of economies on Keynesian principles based around mass production (which will be covered next). Although originating in the inflationary problems of the 1970s, the second form of globalisation came through neoliberal economics, was implemented in the 1980s. Led by Margaret Thatcher and Ronald Reagan, national governments chose to deregulate their economies. International organisations were used to enforce these rules, including GATT, the IMF and World Bank. The formation of the EU was part of this wider process and implemented free market economics on member states. The wider impact of these policies resulted in a dramatic transformation of the types of jobs that were found in the UK, US and across Europe. As national economies shifted from national control based around mass manufacturing, neoliberal economies focused on knowledge and information in the service sectors.

Post-industrialisation

The motorcar became the main driver (pun intended) of national economies after the Second World War. After the UK's EU referendum, more focus was placed on the fact that Nissan and Honda were closing manufacturing in Sunderland and Swindon than on other job losses. The importance of the car factory in the UK (note they are not British companies, but Japanese) is not just because it is often a large local employer, but also because the car has become a metaphor for post-war society. The road movie has become the romantic expression of individual freedom as the protagonists find themselves on a haphazard adventure of self-discovery. Elsewhere the washed and polished car in the driveway becomes the symbol of suburban respectability. The car allowed the burgeoning middle classes to flee the city and buy larger properties away from the intensity of the inner cities. In contrast to this image of decency, the sleek sports car has become a symbol of masculinity; the image of power and independence. Not only has the car come to symbolise consumption in Western society, but it has also underpinned our understandings of post-war production. As the industrial production of commodities like cars have changed, so has the society that has developed around it.

The interventionist approaches advocated by John Maynard Keynes required a consistent demand and secure employment. Mass manufacturing provided a solution to this approach and the car industry was the prototype. In particular this model was based around Fordism, the industrial organisation of the Ford motor corporation (see Box 7.3). Henry Ford, the company's founder, drew on the work of US mechanical engineer Frederick Taylor, whose *Principles of Scientific Management* (1911) proposed a technique of labour discipline and workplace organisation based on 'scientific' studies of human efficiency and incentive systems. This extended the division of labour proposed by Adam Smith and sought to make workers as efficient as possible. The techniques were not restricted to capitalist societies, but were also introduced into the Soviet Union as a means of providing full employment.

Fordist manufacturing was enabled by state policies. As the Bretton Woods agreement ensured managed national markets, national governments would control tariffs and exchange rates to ensure that national industries were protected and kept their employees in work. Political support was also needed to permit the building of massive factories; in some cases, state subsidies were provided to allow factories to move around the country and to ensure jobs were available for the local population. Support was also required from the state for the wider infrastructure, such as roads. It was not good for these industries if there were still dirt tracks around the country.

In the UK there became a 'post-war consensus' (Addison, 1975) between the Labour and Conservative parties that maintained this approach. Both parties effectively agreed to employ Keynesian

Box 7.3: Fordism

Fordism was a term proposed by the Italian Marxist theorist Antonio Gramsci. It was extended to account for the broader organisation of industry, the economy and by extension wider society. Within the factories of Ford, it meant the reorganisation of the entire productive process by means of the moving assembly line, standardisation, and, importantly for society, a mass market. Fordism is an economic philosophy in which prosperity and high corporate profits are achieved by means of high wages that allow the workers to purchase the output they produce, such as automobiles. It is also underpinned and supported by the state; industry and the state work in tandem. Within the factories, Fordism is a hierarchical organisation with each part of the process devolved to semi-skilled workers who would perform the same repetitive task over and over again. The jobs were invariably boring. In order to compensate workers, Henry Ford would pay his staff more. This had the added bonus of enabling his workers to buy the very cars that they were making. In effect, they became advertisers of his products. George Ritzer has suggested that Fordist, rational production remains in place today. In his book entitled *The McDonaldization of Society* (1993), Ritzer argues that society is increasingly organised like a McDonalds restaurant in that it is standardised. Ritzer builds on Max Weber's notion of 'rationalisation' by suggesting that global capitalism is increasingly rational, bureaucratic and looking for efficiency. McDonalds' burgers are the same shape with the same ingredients. Like the Ford car, there was a limited, but standard set of options that the customer could purchase. McDonalds' restaurants are similar throughout the world. This leads to a more homogeneous and uniform world. Despite this, there are national differences and McDonalds has diversified to account for this.

policies and support this form of industrial policy alongside a welfare state. The development of the welfare state (see Box 7.4) was more of a European phenomenon than a US one, partly because of a much stronger tradition of state control. Fordism becomes a way of life, spilling over into lifestyle and culture. Higher wages, stable employment, and cheaper consumer products led to an increasingly affluent society. Across North America and Western Europe, various economic 'miracles' provided similar consumption booms. In the US and the UK there was a growing suburbanisation as the working and middle classes moved from the cities to the suburbs. They could afford the cars that allowed them to commute as well as the various material objects that symbolised a comfortable life, such as washing machines and televisions. Youth subcultures also flourished as young people could afford to purchase their own clothes and lifestyle (as we saw in Chapter 2).

Fordism was based on a set on presumptions that started to collapse in the 1970s. The wider global economic climate was beginning to challenge national control of markets thanks to Richard Nixon

Box 7.4: The development of the UK welfare system

After the Second World War, both the Labour and Conservative parties acknowledged the need to establish a welfare state. In the UK, the Beveridge Report (1942) established the British welfare system. Beveridge wanted to tackle the five evils with a 'war on want, disease, ignorance, squalor and idleness'. This was to be achieved through 'support from the cradle to the grave' in the form of social insurance, NHS and education. These would provide educated and healthy workers for the industries and protect them should they face redundancy. The Beveridge Report laid the foundation for welfare provision in the UK and acted as the social provision to Keynesian economic policies. The key provisions related to health, housing, unemployment, child support and pensions.

uncoupling the US dollar from the gold standard. The rise in oil prices clearly had a dramatic impact on national economies based on car manufacturing. These large corporations were also starting to become multinationals and looking to trade globally. The principles were also based on the idea of a nuclear family (which we covered in Chapter 6) that was beginning to be challenged in the 1970s. Moreover, the lifecycle began to change with the school leaving age, retirement age and life expectancy all changing. As people's health improved thanks to the NHS and better nutrition, the population lived longer and this meant more of a strain on the state pension. The more comfortable society started to show the pressure after the global economic crisis of the 1970s. Full employment had meant strong trade unions. Yet Keynesian economics meant that wages needed to be controlled to prevent inflation. As inflation rose in the wake of the Nixon shock and the oil crisis, wages were capped, but prices were rising. This led to strikes and rising unemployment from businesses affected by the global crisis. There was also growing political agitation from a range of areas, including 'Women's Lib', civil rights, student movements and environmental groups.

The collapse of the Keynesian system had a dramatic impact on Fordism. A new form of automobile manufacturing that was perfected in Japan also precipitated this transformation. What could be called post-Fordism was a way of organising assembly lines to give more autonomy to individual workers. The old Fordist assembly lines were incredibly hierarchical and workers would have to defer to a manager if they wanted to stop the line. As this incurred substantial cost, managers rarely permitted this. The result was that quality suffered as any mistakes in production could only be rectified at the end of the process. As detailed in *The Machine That Changed The World* (Womack et al, 1991), the owner of Toyota, Eiji Toyoda had studied the Fordist principles in the US, but identified the poor quality and costly rectification process as inefficient. He also observed that being competitive in the market couldn't be achieved through treating workers like machines. A system of lean manufacturing was perfected where the assembly workers were seen as the experts. They were given complete autonomy to stop the line should they identify a problem. They were also part of the discussion, or quality circle, to find a solution to the problem. Over time, problems were ironed out of the process and quality dramatically improved. Assembly lines also changed as workers became teams of specialists responsible for a range of functions. Technology also led to many repetitive tasks being automated. The result was a smaller but more skilled workforce.

With fewer manufacturing problems, there was less of a requirement to hold significant stock. Max Weber's idea that capitalism was constantly striving for 'rationalisation' and efficiencies could be seen in how stock was managed. A system of 'just-in-time' storage was implemented, which meant that stock was brought into the factory 'just in time' for use on the assembly line. This meant that the company did not have to pay to keep stock in their warehouse. This required more cooperation with their suppliers. Under Fordism, management was hierarchical and secretive. Under the lean manufacturing of Toyota, they were open about their requirements and invited their suppliers to provide solutions to problems. This process was also witnessed in Italy with the small manufacturers in the Emila-Romagna region (Piore and Sabel, 1984). Greater cooperation between competitors and suppliers meant that each company became smaller and more efficient, as well as producing better quality products.

Hidden social relations that impact on how we live our everyday lives, like Fordism and other industrial transformations, extend well beyond the process of engineering. It is not simply about how we produce things, but also how we consume and how we organise our lives. It reflects the decreasing importance of scale. Companies are seeking to be lean and efficient. It is driven by changes in communications, logistics and information technology (IT). Computers ensure that stock can arrive on the factory floor or in the shops at the most efficient time. More importantly they cooperate to ensure efficiency. Silicon Valley is a good example of a range of high-technology enterprises operating in one area, who cooperate together. The nature of IT requires participants in this economic environment to operate across all platforms. Facebook,

Google and other software developers need to be able to work with Apple, Microsoft and Unix, and vice versa.

The other impact of post-Fordism is on employment. In Western Europe and North America, there is no longer a requirement for low skilled workers. This work can be outsourced to countries like China. Where industrial societies are organised around differences between labour and capital, post-industrial society is organised around differences of education. As US sociologist Daniel Bell (1973: 212) says, 'The post-industrial society … is a knowledge society'. Elsewhere French sociologist Alain Touraine (1971) has suggested that this is a 'technocratic' or 'programmed society'. Technical knowledge helps organise and shape the economy and society. As the economy has restructured since the 1980s, a 'service economy' has emerged. Jobs that require technical and professional skills now play a more important role in society and the economy than manual occupations. The majority of the labour force now works in areas such as research and development, legal and financial services, education, health, IT and marketing. These are the people that produce, organise and then apply knowledge. Even in the production industry, these are the skills required to organise the production runs and ensure that the automation lines keep running. There has been a consequent expansion of universities to produce and extend this knowledge.

The expansion of middle management, particularly throughout the decades after the Second World War, contributed to this growth in a knowledge economy. This 'managerial revolution' (Bell, 1973), shifted the power of shareholders and owners. As businesses developed, they attracted more shareholders as investors. Yet this made it harder for owners, particularly family shareholders, to maintain control. Bankers played a key role in financing these investments, particularly through acquisitions and mergers, and this helped to remove the old family shareholders from the top management positions. In their place came a class of professional managers whose knowledge and technical ability developed the businesses. This managerial revolution had a dramatic influence on class. No longer was there a clear class division between capitalist owners and their workers, as Marx argued (and as was discussed in Chapter 4). A new knowledge-based class structure emerged. Teachers, professors, engineers, accountants and lawyers emerged to fulfil the roles of the changing economy. Those without the technical knowledge or education are excluded from positions of power and are seen as 'dependent participation' (Touraine, 1971: 9).

The restructuring of the global economy has been facilitated by IT. Spanish sociologist Manuel Castells argues that the growing and intensifying IT revolution is restructuring capitalism on a global level (globalisation). It is also seeing a resurgence of old forms of identity like nationalism and new forms of new social movements. Castells is keen to highlight that the IT revolution did not create his 'network society', but it would be impossible to exist without it. Companies, institutions and individuals gain competitiveness and productivity from information and the technology used to process and exchange information. Although this can lead to greater interaction and cooperation, it can also be exclusionary.

This new informational economy is global. However, this economy is fragmented and becoming regionalised. There is an uneven geography to this economy. Thanks to IT there are increased flows of people, capital and information between places, in particular into cities. Dutch sociologist Saskia Sassen (2001) has highlighted that there are a number of global cities that stand apart from their nation as they accumulate resources and monopolise these flows of people, capital and information. New York, London and Tokyo are good examples, but regional and local cities are also emerging, like Atlanta, Barcelona and Manchester. Here, cities have usurped the nation state and operate as nodes in a global network. As production has been outsourced to countries with cheaper labour costs, the research and development, finance, legal services and marketing remain in the global cities. Head offices are located in these cities as they are cities with a range of consumer possibilities. London has the Royal Opera House, museums, theatres, a number of Premier League football clubs, Twickenham, Lords, the Oval and any number of quality restaurants and shops. The directors and workers in the corporate headquarters have a city which provides services for their economic and cultural capital.

The city becomes a hub of service production and accumulates more power accordingly. In this way cities can market themselves and brand themselves. After the 2016 EU referendum there were strong calls for London to establish itself as a city state. While observing the London 2012 Olympic Games, it was possible to see how London was selling itself to the global marketplace. For Castells (1996: 386), the

> global city is not a place, but a process. A process by which centres of production and consumption of advanced services, and their ancillary local societies, are connected in a global network, while simultaneously downplaying the linkages with their hinterlands on the basis of information flows.

A global city is connected to other global cities with the required information, knowledge and skills. Yet they are not connected to other cities and towns in the same way. As de-industrialisation has occurred and many towns and cities in the UK have become post-industrial, they no longer have the skills required in the global marketplace. Yet they also don't have the services or skills that investors want, which can be found elsewhere in the world. As neoliberal governments do not see their duty as intervening in the market, then these locations become separated from the wider economy.

Having a sociological imagination helps show that many of these problems are independent of the EU. Yet the EU became the symbol of the wider changes in British society as a result of globalisation. The polarisation that has taken place in the UK between new global cities and post-industrial towns and cities was starkly revealed in the EU referendum result. Manchester, London and smaller cities with strong knowledge-based and creative economies such as Bristol and Brighton & Hove all voted overwhelmingly to remain in the EU. These cities have the workers with the skills and knowledge that are succeeding in the global economy. Post-industrial towns and cities in the North, Midlands and South West have disproportionately suffered as a result of globalisation. The referendum represented an opportunity to 'take back control'. The problem is that the EU is not the architect, nor the cause of the problems they face. These towns and cities will probably fare much worse as a result of leaving the EU: they will no longer receive EU funding set aside to mitigate the problems of uneven globalisation (which the UK government does not cover). Meanwhile, the global cities will still have a workforce with skills that are required in the global marketplace. Sociology helps explain these wider political, economic and social processes that impact on the individuals' life.

KEY POINTS SUMMARY

- Political economy is the relationship between politics and economics. Even under economic theories like neoliberalism, which argue for limited government involvement in the economy, the state still has a role to play in managing the economy or the effects of the economy.
- The post-war period in the UK was characterised by the post-war consensus where both political parties agreed to uphold Keynesianism, which aimed for full employment, allowed state support for industries and was underpinned by the welfare state.
- Since the 1980s, economic policies in the UK have followed neoliberalism, which argues for minimal state involvement in economics, other than supporting private property and policing the effects of policies. Neoliberalism is characterised by a push towards individual responsibility, deregulation of social policies and privatisation, which pushes for all aspects of everyday life to be open to the free market.
- Globalisation is a long process that has seen connections across the globe shrink. It has brought more people into contact with people from across the globe, as well as seeing businesses relocate, goods and services being sold globally, and people migrating. Each of these has economic, social and cultural impacts on people in diverse locations around the world.

KEY READING GUIDE

- The ever-expanding predictability of consumption was outlined by George Ritzer in *The McDonaldization of Society* (1993). He argues that the constant drive for efficiency in production results in predictability, just like a McDonalds restaurant, which effectively means consumers are becoming homogenised across the world.
- In *Global Cities: New York, London, Tokyo* (1991) Saskia Sassen argues that cities are the new powerhouses of economies. Corporate headquarters remain in these global cities where the directors and executives can continue to be close to sources of capital (investors), ideas and spaces of consumption. This creates an uneven geography of employment and opportunity.
- There are many books on the concept of globalisation. Many will take the disciplinary perspective of the author (political scientists will focus on politics, anthropologists on culture, and so on). Roland Robertson's *Globalization: Social Theory and Global Culture* (1992) synthesises the various historical, economic, political and cultural aspects into one collective approach.

8

The UK in the future

Through a brief exploration of some features of everyday life, we have covered over 60 years of British history, gone global, and tackled big issues like race, gender, sexuality and class, as well as touched on national and international processes like globalisation and the UK referendum on leaving the EU. This book has introduced some of the key thinkers and conceptual arguments in the field of sociology and hopefully shown that there is no definitive answer. Even with a sociological imagination there are different analyses and interpretations of global and local events and social processes. Where some sociologists argue that there is growing individualisation in society, others believe we are still fundamentally social animals, constantly forming new friendships, groups, collectives and social movements. As outlined in the introductory chapter, US sociologist Randall Collins (1998: 3) said, 'There is literally nothing you can't see in a fresh way if you turn your sociological eye to it. Being a sociologist means never having to be bored.' Hopefully we've fired your sociological imagination and encouraged a new way of looking at the world.

This is only a short guide. It is not intended to be *the* definitive guide, nor the only discussion and analysis of complex topics. Sociology is a broad subject. It has to be, as it is concerned with the infinitely interesting and changeable animal that we call humans. Throughout history, humans have engaged in all sorts of social activities. But even fundamental human activities like sex, love and relationships have changed over time. Even though the book has argued that we live in a global world, there are still innumerable differences between social groups across the globe. Even something as ubiquitous as football has a myriad of different ways of playing, organising and supporting. I hope that the book has given you an insight into thinking sociologically and helps you to critically engage with the world around you.

The key things to consider when thinking sociologically are:

- Social life is intimately and complexly interconnected, particularly in a globalised world. Events that occur thousands of miles away can have an immeasurable impact on those in the UK, for example; conflict in the Middle East can trigger mass migration of refugees in Europe.
- Our lives oscillate between having some control, or agency, over our choices and being structured by wider social, political and economic forces. This debate between structure and agency is a constant debate within sociology.
- Sociologists use a range of methods to gather evidence and then apply this to, and in turn develop, broader social theories like political economy, critical race theory or feminism. In this way we ground these theories with empirical data, rather than simply being that bloke down the pub who has an opinion about everything without sufficient, robust evidence to back it.
- The 'sociological eye' is varied. There are many different ways of looking at the world sociologically. We have chosen to do so through everyday life. We could place political economy, class, race, sexuality or gender central in the analysis. We could use any number of everyday practices to understand wider society. Subdivisions of sociology on religion, sport, intimacy, death, consumption, science, art and others all provide us with an opportunity to understand the social world around us.
- Life is not 'common sense'. Common sense manages to combine two significant aspects of sociology – the self and society. Merely stating something to be a 'fact' or 'common sense' because it is my own experience is placing myself at the centre of the universe. It does not consider other possibilities. If it is 'common sense'

because other people like me think the same, then this is socially determined, but no less problematic. Indeed, a commitment to 'common sense' can be ideological, particularly when it becomes a barrier to changing the status quo.

• A sociological imagination needs to consider *all* sides to the argument, not just privilege one's own view or that of one's immediate family and friends. Alvin Gouldner (1968) calls this 'underdog sociology'. We don't have to take sides (as Howard Becker suggested), but we have a duty to present all sides. In this way we get to understand our own perspectives and assumptions as well as those of others.

• Sociologists have to be reflective. Just because someone has not experienced something – like racism, sexism, or ableism – does not mean that these things do not exist.

• Sociology is the 'art of listening', as Les Back argues (2007). By listening to the experiences of others, we develop our sociological imagination.

• Sociology, like social life, is emotional. Humans are emotional animals and we act according to these emotions. It is important to understand why people fear losing their jobs to immigrants, or why they are ecstatic when their football team wins a match. These emotions help us to understand why people act in certain ways.

Sociology in the future

To paraphrase the British novelist L.P. Hartley, 'the future is another country; they do things differently there.' For some, that breeds uncertainty and risk; for others it can be exciting – a voyage into the unknown. Sociology gives us the skills and knowledge to make sense of the world, whichever direction it goes in. The future is uncertain, but developing our sociological imagination will help us navigate those uncertainties. This section draws out some themes we think will impact society in the future.

- Questions of race, gender, class and sexuality will continue to dominate the discipline of sociology. These are central to many people's identity, and as such, will remain the core of sociological inquiry. We think these will develop in two ways. One is that a more intersectional approach will continue as the experience of, for instance, a young gay black man will differ from an older heterosexual Bangladeshi woman. More focus will come to those groups who rarely get analysed, namely those in power. Studies of whiteness, masculinity, middle classes and heterosexuality will emerge so we have a fuller understanding of society.
- The UK's decision to leave the EU will continue to prompt discussions in Europe and its impact will ripple out globally as the withdrawal of the UK from the EU gets underway.
- Across the globe, ethno-nationalist politicians (for example Donald Trump in the US, Jair Bolsonaro in Brazil, Narendra Modi in India, Recep Tayyip Erdoğan in Turkey, Vladimir Putin in Russia and Rodrigo Duterte in the Philippines) have won and continue to hang onto power; this will shape global politics, economy and society.
- Globalisation is affected by decisions by global politicians, but also transnational corporations and local populations. What, how and where businesses want to sell will impact what we can buy. Similarly, what we demand as increasingly socially conscious consumers can have some influence on how we interlink across the globe.
- Global climate change will have a dramatic impact on many communities across the globe. Extreme weather will affect where and how people can live, and its ill effects will be felt across both the southern and northern hemispheres.
- Migration will continue to be a core aspect of sociological concern. Humans are a mobile animal and have always moved. Colonisation and decolonisation have seen millions of people move across the world to colonise, with others moving in the other direction. The numbers of refugees will continue to grow due to war, climate change and poverty; forced migration will

have a dramatic and tragic impact not only on those moving but also on the countries and communities they move to.

- Technology is a key feature of the post-industrial economy. How the internet, social media and other forms of information technology develop will determine the future. Technology has displaced some manual labour and middle-class service sector jobs. We are already seeing automation in everyday life with self-service checkouts in all supermarkets. Driverless cars are being piloted and computer technology will allow the automation of many repetitive service industries. Having the right skills and education to flourish in this new work environment will be key to how individuals and communities survive.

- The repercussion of transformations to work will be changes to leisure and consumption. What we do in our spare time will be determined by where we live and work, and will also affect demand for services.

- The health of Western nations has benefited from post-war economic settlement. More people have access to better nutrition and healthcare resulting in changing demands on healthcare systems. More people are living longer, which impacts on the demands of the welfare state to provide for the retired population. Most European populations are ageing, which will require immigration to maintain current economic development, or a reconfiguration of local and national economies alongside a rehaul of social care systems.

- One knock-on effect of the economic development of the West is the relationship of land to the economy. Many properties are seen as investments, rather than homes or places of work. Housing prices have dramatically increased as a percentage of salary, particularly in cities, and this will impact on how, with whom and where people live.

- In a world that many people feel is changing beyond their control, alternative forms of rootedness can be sought. Potentially, this will see the re-emergence of religion or new forms of spirituality. As people seek to make sense of the world in which they live, some people will look to alternative frameworks of understanding.

- Social groups are not fixed nor remain the same over time, as this book has highlighted. In the past 40 years, older forms of collective behaviour have fragmented. This does not mean that we have become more individualised, as some commentators argue. Instead we have formed new groups, subcultures and communities. The future will see many new and alternative forms of collectivism emerge, all of which will provide the sociologist with a rich, engaged and sensual insight into the future.

Ultimately, this book has argued three main points: first, that humans continue to form new and exciting groups; second, that social inequalities persist despite these changes; and third, that we can learn about ourselves as individuals by understanding wider society. The future will give us an infinite range of everyday activities, interactions and structural changes that will give those with the sociological eye any number of imaginative lines of enquiry. By being aware of the everyday and the underlying social relations, sociologists can be prepared for the future. Society will continue to fragment and realign depending on social, political and economic changes. Despite these changes, some groups will continue to be excluded and struggle to enter certain sections of society. And within all this, those with the sociological imagination will be able to link their own biography, wider history and social changes to link their own 'personal troubles' to 'public issues'. It is hoped that as feminists have successfully done, you will make 'the personal political' and feed this sociological imagination back into society to make it better. Whatever happens, the future will not be boring for sociologists.

References

Addison, P. (1975) *The Road to 1945: British Politics and the Second World War*. Revised edition. London: Cape.

Anderson, B. (2013) *Us and Them? The Dangerous Politics of Immigration Controls*. Oxford: Oxford University Press.

Back, L. (2007) *The Art of Listening*. Oxford and New York: Berg.

Barthes, R. (1993 [1957]) *Mythologies*. London: Vintage.

Beck, U. (1992) *Risk Society*. London: Sage.

Beck, U. and Beck-Gernsheim, E. (1995) *The Normal Chaos of Love*. Cambridge: Polity Press.

Beck, U. and Beck-Gernsheim, E. (2002) *Individualization: Institutionalized Individualism and its Social and Political Consequences*. London: Sage.

Becker, H. (1963) *Outsiders: Studies in the Sociology of Deviance*. New York: Free Press of Glencoe.

Becker, H. (1967) 'Whose side are we on?', *Social Problems*, 14(3): 239–47.

Bell, D. (1973) *The Coming of the Post-Industrial Society*. New York: Basic Books.

Bennett, A. and Kahn-Harris, K. (2004) *After Subculture: Critical Studies in Contemporary Youth Culture*. Basingstoke: Palgrave Macmillan.

Bhambra, G. (2014) *Connected Sociologies*. London: Bloomsbury.

Bobo, L. D. (2011) 'Somewhere between Jim Crow & post-racialism: reflections on the racial divide in America today' *Daedelus*, 140(2): 11–36.

Bogaert, A. (2015) *Understanding Asexuality*. Lanham, MD: Rowman and Littlefield.

Bonilla-Silva, E. (2006) *Racism without Racists: Colorblind Racism and the Persistence of Racial Inequality in the United States*. Lanham: Rowman and Littlefield.

Bourdieu, P. (1984) *Distinction: A Social Critique of the Judgement of Taste*. Cambridge, MA: Harvard University Press.

Brah, A. (1996) *Cartographies of Diaspora: Contesting Identities*. London and New York: Routledge.

Burkhalter B (2006) 'Anomalies and ambiguities: finding and discounting the relevance of race in interracial relationships', in P. Drew, G. Raymond and D. Weinberg (eds), *Talk and Interaction in Social Research Methods*, London: SAGE, pp 171–89.

Butler, J. (1990) *Gender Trouble: Feminism and the Subversion of Identity*. London: Routledge.

Bryman, A. (2012) *Social Research Methods*. Oxford: Oxford University Press.

Carrington, B. (2010) *Race, Sport and the Sporting Black Diaspora*. London: Sage.

Carter, J. (2013) 'The curious absence of love stories in women's talk', *The Sociological Review*, 61(4): 728–44.

Castells, M. (1996) *The Rise of the Network Society*. Oxford: Blackwell.

Castles, S. (2000) *Ethnicity and Globalization*. London: Sage.

Castles, S. (2009) *The Age of Migration: International Population Movements in the Modern World*. Basingstoke: Palgrave Macmillan.

Cohen, S. (1972) *Folk Devils and Moral Panics*. London: MacGibbon and Key.

Cohen, S.B. (2006) 'Borat: Cultural Learnings of America for Make Benefit Glorious Nation of Kazakhstan'. Directed by Larry Charles. [Film] Los Angeles: 20th Century Fox.

Collins, P.H. (1990) *Black Feminist Thought*. Boston, MA. Unwin Hyman.

Collins, R. (1998) 'The sociological eye and its blinders', *Contemporary Sociology*, 27(1): 2–7.

Comer, L. (1974) *Wedlocked Women*. New York: Feminist Press.

Connell, R.W. (1987) *Gender and Power. Society, the Person and Sexual Politics*. New York: Polity Press.

Connell, R.W. (1995) *Masculinities*. Berkley, CA: University of California Press.

Crenshaw, K. (1989) 'Demarginalizing the intersection of race and sex: a black feminist critique of antidiscrimination doctrine, feminist theory and antiracist politics', *University of Chicago Legal Forum*, 1989(1): 139–67.

Davis, A. (1981) *Women, Race and Class*. New York: Random House.

de Beauvoir, S. (1949) *The Second Sex*. London: Penguin.

D'Onofrio, L. and Munk, K. (2004) *Understanding the Stranger*. London: ICAR.

Dorling, D. (2016) Brexit: the decision of a divided country. *British Medical Journal* 354: i3697.

Du Bois, W.E.B. (1903) *Souls of Black Folk*. Oxford: Oxford University Press.

Dunscombe, J. and Marsden, D. (1993) 'Love and intimacy: the gender division of emotion and 'emotion work': a neglected aspect of sociological discussion of heterosexual relationships', *Sociology*, 27(2): 221–41.

Dzodan, F. (2011) 'My feminism will be intersectional or it will be bullshit', http://tigerbeatdown.com/2011/10/10/my-feminism-will-be-intersectional-or-it-will-be-bullshit/

Elias, N. (1978) *What is Sociology?* New York: Columbia University Press.

Ferguson, N. (2003) *Empire*. London: Penguin.

Flanagan, M. (2009) 'Micky Flanagan: What Chance Change?' BBC Radio 4, 6 January.

Friday, N. (1973) *My Secret Garden*. New York: Trident Press.

Friedan, B. (1963) *The Feminine Mystique*. Oxford: Norton & Co.

Friedman, M. (1962) *Capitalism and Freedom*. Chicago: University of Chicago Press.

Friedman, M. (1963) *A Monetary History of the United States*. Princeton: Princeton University Press.

Garfinkel, H. (1967) *Studies in Ethnomethodology*. Cambridge: Polity Press.

Giddens, A. (1990) *The Consequences of Modernity*. Stanford: Stanford University Press.

Giddens, A. (1991) *Modernity and Self-identity*. Stanford: Stanford University Press.

Giddens, A. (1992) *The Transformation of Intimacy*. New York: Wiley.

Gilpin, R. (2001) *Global Political Economy: Understanding the International Order*. Princeton: Princeton University Press.

Gilroy, P. (1987) *There Ain't No Black in the Union Jack*. London: Unwin Hyman.

Gilroy, P. (1993) *The Black Atlantic: Modernity and Double Consciousness*. London and New York: Verso.

Goffman, A. (2014) *On the Run: Fugitive Life in an American City*. Chicago: University of Chicago Press.

Goffman, E. (1959) *The Presentation of Self in Everyday Life*, London: Penguin Random House.

Goldberg, D.T. (2009) *The Threat of Race*. Malden: Blackwell.

Goldin, C. and Rouse, C. (2000) 'Orchestrating impartiality: the impact of "blind" auditions on female musicians', *American Economic Review*, 90(4): 715–41.

Gouldner, A. (1968) 'The sociologist as partisan: sociology and the welfare state', *The American Sociologist*, 3(2): 103–16.

Gramsci, A. (1971) *Selections from the Prison Notebooks of Antonio Gramsci*. London: Lawrence & Wishart.

Greer, G. (1970) *The Female Eunuch*. London: Paladin.

Hall, S. (1991) 'Old and new identities, old and new ethnicities', in A.D. King (ed), *Culture, Globalization and the World-System: Contemporary Conditions for the Representation of Identity*. Basingstoke: Macmillan.

Hall, S. (1996) 'Who needs "identity"?' In S. Hall and P. Du Gay (eds) *Questions of Cultural Identity*. London: Sage, pp 1-17.

Hall, S. and Jefferson, T. (1976) *Resistance Through Rituals, Youth Subcultures in Post-War Britain*. London: Hutchinson.

Hatton, T.J. and Williamson, J.G. (1998) *The Age of Mass Migration: Causes and Economic Impact*. Oxford: Oxford University Press.

Hayek, F. (1944) *The Road to Serfdom*. Chicago: University of Chicago Press.

Hebdige, D. (1976) Reggae, Rastas and Rudies, in S. Hall and T. Jefferson (eds) *Resistance Through Rituals: Youth Subcultures in Post-War Britain*, London: Hutchinson, pp 113–28.

Hebdige, D. (1979) *Subculture: The Meaning of Style*. London and New York: Routledge.

Held, D. (2000) *Global Transformations*. Cambridge: Polity Press.

Hochlaf, D. and Franklin, B. (2016) *Immigration: Encourage or Deter?* London: International Longevity Centre.

Hochschild, A. (1983) *The Managed Heart: Commercialization of Human Feeling*. Berkley: University of California Press.

Hochschild, A. (2003) *The Commercialisation of Intimate Life*. Berkley: University of California Press.

Hodkinson, P. (2002) *Goth. Identity, Style and Subculture Dress, Body, Culture*. London: Berg.

hooks, b. (1984) *Feminist Theory: From Margin to Centre*. Boston, MA. South End Press.

Horne, J. and Whannel, G. (2012) *Understanding the Olympics*. London and New York: Routledge.

Hunter, R.D. (2012) 'Reginald D. Hunter Live'. [DVD] London: Universal Pictures.

Jackson, S. (1996) 'Sexual skirmishes and feminist factions: twenty-five years of debate on women and sexuality', in S. Jackson and S. Scott (eds), *Feminism and Sexuality: A Reader*, Edinburgh/New York: Edinburgh University Press/Columbia University Press, pp 1–31.

James, C.L.R. (1963) *Beyond a Boundary*. London: Hutchinson.

Jamieson, L. (1998) *Intimacy: Personal Relationships in Modern Societies*. Cambridge: Polity Press.

Jones, O. (2011) *Chavs: The Demonisation of the Working Class*. London: Verso.

Keynes, J.M. (1936) *The General Theory of Employment, Interest and Money*. London: Macmillan.

Klinenberg, E. (2012) *Going Solo: The Extraordinary Rise and Surprising Appeal of Living Alone*. London: Penguin.

Macpherson, W. (1999) *The Stephen Lawrence Inquiry: Report of an Inquiry by Sir William Macpherson*. London: Home Office.

Maffesoli, M. (1996) *The Time of the Tribes*. London: Sage.

Marx, K. and Engels, F. (1948) *The Communist Manifesto*. London: Penguin.

McDonald, I. and Billings, P. (2007) 'The treatment of asylum seekers in the UK', *Journal of Social Welfare and Family Law*, 29(1): 49–65.

McDowell, L. (2000) 'The trouble with men? Young people, gender transformations and the crisis of masculinity', *International Journal of Urban and Regional Research*, 24(1): 201–9.

McKenzie, L. (2015) *Getting By*. Bristol: Policy Press.

McRobbie, A. (2009) *The Aftermath of Feminism: Gender Culture, and Social Change*. London: Sage.

McRobbie, A. and Garber, J. (1976) 'Girls and subcultures', in S. Hall and T. Jefferson (eds), *Resistance Through Rituals: Youth Subcultures in Post-War Britain*, London: Hutchinson, pp 209–23.

Mead, G.H. (1934) *Mind, Self and Society*. Chicago: Chicago University Press.

Meštrović, S. (1997) *Postemotional Society*. London: Sage.

Mills, C.W. (1959) *The Sociological Imagination*. Oxford: Oxford University Press.

Murray, C. (1990) *The Emerging British Underclass*. London: Institute of Economic Affairs.

Nicholson, R. (2013) 'Bridget Christie: "I've a long way to go."' *The Guardian*, 28 August. https://www.theguardian.com/culture/2013/aug/28/bridget-christie-edinburgh-comedy-award.

Oakley, A. (1972) *Sex, Gender and Society*. New York: Harper & Row.

Oakley, A. (1974) *Housewife*. London. Allen Lane.

O'Hara, M. (2014) *Austerity Bites*. Bristol: Policy Press.

Orbach, S. (1981) *Fat is a Feminist Issue*. London: Hamlyn.

Papastergiadis, N. (2000) *The Turbulence of Migration: Globalization, Deterritorialization and Hybridity*. Cambridge: Polity Press.

Parsons, T. (1955) *Family, Socialization and Interaction Process*. New York: New York Free Press.

Pearson, G. (1983) *Hooligan: A History of Respectable Fears*. London: Macmillan.

Phipps, A. and Young, I. (2015) 'Neoliberalisation and "lad cultures" in higher education', *Sociology*, 49(2): 305–22.

Piore, M. and Sabel, C. (1984) *The Second Industrial Divide*. New York: Basic Books.

Plummer, K. (1995) *Telling Sexual Stories*. London: Routledge.

Putnam, R.D. (2000) *Bowling Alone: The Collapse and Revival of American Community*. New York: Simon and Schuster.

Rich, A. (1980) 'Compulsory heterosexuality and the lesbian existence', *Signs*, 5(4): 631–60.

Riesman, D. (1950) *The Lonely Crowd: A Study of Changing American Character*. New Haven: Yale University Press.

Ritzer, G. (1993) *The McDonaldization of Society*. Thousand Oaks: Pine Forge Press.

Rubin, G. (1975) 'The traffic in women: notes on the "political economy" of sex', in R. Reiter (ed), *Toward an Anthropology of Women*, New York: Monthly Review Press, pp 157–210.

Robertson, R. (1992) *Globalization*. London: Sage.

Saini, A. (2019) *Superior: The Return of Race Science*. London: 4th Estate.

Sassen, S. (2001) *The Global City: New York, London, Tokyo*. Princeton: Princeton University Press.

Savage, M. (2015) *Social Class in the 21st Century*. London: Pelican Books.

Sian, K. (2019) *Navigating Institutional Racism in British Universities*. London: Palgrave Macmillan.

Simmel, G. (1950) *The Sociology of George Simmel*. London: Free Press of Glencoe.

Skeggs, B. (1997) *Formations of Class and Gender*. London: Sage.

Skeggs, B. (2004) *Class, Self and Culture*. London: Routledge.

Smit, B. (2006) *Pitch Invasion: Adidas, Puma and the Making of Modern Sport*. London: Penguin.

Smith, A. (2008 [1776]) *The Wealth of Nations*. Oxford: Oxford University Press.

Smith, D.E. (1987) *The Everyday World as Problematic: A Feminist Sociology*. Boston: Northeastern University Press.

Solomos, J. (2003) *Race and Racism in Britain*. Basingstoke: Palgrave Macmillan.

Stacey, J. (1996) *In the Name of the Family: Rethinking Family Values in the Postmodern Age*. Boston, MA: Beacon Press.

Standing, G. (2011) *The Precariat: the new dangerous class*. London: Bloomsbury Academic.

Sugden, J. and Tomlinson, A. (1999) *FIFA and the Conquest for World Football*. Cambridge: Polity Press.

Taylor, F. (1911) *Principles of Scientific Management*. London: Harper.

Tharoor, S. (2017) *Inglorious Empire*. London: Penguin.

Thornton, S. (1995) *Club Cultures*. Cambridge: Polity Press.

Touraine, A. (1971) *The Post-Industrial Society. Tomorrow's Social History: Classes, Conflicts and Culture in the Programmed Society*. New York: Random House.

Twamley, K., Doidge, M. and Scott, A. (2015) *Sociologists' Tales*. Bristol: Policy Press.

Tyler, I. (2013) 'The riots of the underclass? Stigmatisation, mediation and the government of poverty and disadvantage in neoliberal Britain', *Sociological Research Online*, 18(4) 6, www.socresonline.org.uk/18/4/6.html

Van Hooff, J. (2013) *Modern Couples? Continuity and Change in Heterosexual Relationships*. London: Routledge.

Virdee, S. (2014) *Racism, Class and The Racialized Outsider*. Basingstoke: Palgrave Macmillan.

Wadsworth, J., Dhingra, S., Ottaviano, G. and Van Reenen, J. (2016) *Brexit and the Impact of Immigration on the UK*. London: Centre for Economic Performance.

Weber, M. (1978) *Economy and Society*. Berkeley: University of California Press.

Weber, M. (2001 [1905]) *The Protestant Work Ethic and the Spirit of Capitalism*. Oxford: Oxford University Press.

Weeks, J. (1995) *Invented Moralities*. New York: Columbia University Press.

Weeks, J. (2000) *Making Sexual History*. Cambridge: Polity Press.

Weinberg, M.S., Williams, C.J. and Pryor, D.W. (1995) *Dual Attraction: Understanding Bisexuality*. Oxford: Oxford University Press.

Wheaton, B. (2004) *Understanding Lifestyle Sports: Consumption, Identity, and Difference*. London: Routledge.

Willis, P. (1977) *Learning to Labour: How Working Class Kids get Working Class Jobs*. Farnborough: Saxon House.

Womack, J., Jones, D. and Roos, D. (1991) *The Machine That Changed The World*. New York: Productivity Press.

Yuval-Davis, N. (2011) *The Politics of Belonging: Intersectional Contestations*. London: Sage.

Zolberg, A., Suhrke, A. and Aguayo, S. (1989) *Escape from Violence: Conflict and the Refugee Crisis in the Developing World*. Oxford: Oxford University Press.

Index

Note: Page numbers for figures appear in italics.